THE ADVENTURES OF A
SIXTY-SOMETHING WOMAN

RED HEELS
AND
SMOKIN'

HOW I GOT MY MOXIE BACK

*Get your
moxie on.
Nikki Hanna*

NIKKI HANNA

Published by Patina Publishing
727 S. Norfolk Avenue
Tulsa, Oklahoma 74120

Copyright © 2014 by Nequita Hanna

IBSN: 978-0-9828726-7-3 (print)
ISBN: 978-0-9828726-8-0 (electronic)

Library of Congress Control Number: 2014904575

Manufactured in The United States of America

Photography: Steven Michaels, Tulsa OK
Creative Design: Wayne Kruse, Tulsa OK
Graphic Design: JP Jones, Paige1Media

DEDICATION:

To my children who, when they read my stories, ask, "Did you really do that?"

To my grandchildren, twinkling stars who call me GoGo and believe I am somehow cosmically important and that I live at the airport.

To my girlfriends, who inspire me to write a bad ass book that leaves it all on the table.

ACKNOWLEDGEMENTS:

Thanks to Donna Parsons, Lhonda Harris, Gwen O'Brien, Eloise Crowley, Steven Hall, Cheryl Briggs, Toni Ellis, Cathy Butler, Mona Betz, Gay Martin, John Biggs, Bill Wetterman, Pam Wetterman, Britton Gildersleeve, Christine Matthies, Paul Bevilacqua, Harvey Blumenthal, Mike Newman, David Tinney, Michael McRuiz, George Feller, Maxine Bulechek, Sandra Anderson, and Melanie Corbin for their encouragement and contributions. A special thanks to Wayne Kruse for his creative input.

CONTENTS

—THE RALLY—
RED HEELS AND SMOKIN'

INTRODUCTION

When you turn sixty, you begin to disappear. You can refuse to do so, though. I did. If you are a woman, this book is for you and those who care about you. By the time you finish it, my wish is that my story entertained and inspired you, as it did me in the writing of it. I also hope it encourages you to turn wispy dreams into exhilarating reality. If you are a man, this book may take you to a level of confusion never before experienced.

When I was younger, I never dreamed that in my sixties I would become the best version of myself. I couldn't have envisioned being so excited about turning seventy that at sixty-nine I would throw myself a *Pushing 70* birthday party and boast, "This is what seventy looks like." Nor could I have anticipated that I would view this time as my best time. I couldn't have dreamed that big, and I have not even peaked yet. I am a woman in crescendo.

The path to this state was not smooth. It is not as though I woke up one morning speaking French. It was a decade-long caper. My sixties started in neutral territory, deteriorated into a funk, then blossomed into a spirited adventure. The passage was complicated and thorny, but it changed everything.

After a lifetime of being full of moxie, I entered my sixties thinking I could take whatever the third trimester of life dished out—master it like the challenges of the past. I was unable, though, to conjure up good feelings about rug burns from a fall rather than from an erotic experience. I had no premonition that my sense of relevance would fade, that I would become a voyeur of life rather than a participant in it. As I retired from a flourishing career, a tsunami of problems overwhelmed me, and lost love left me wounded and fragile. I struggled.

Then the aging fairy bitch-slapped me—hard. Although I didn't expect aging to be pleasant, I did not anticipate a transformation so flush with vulnerabilities that I would drown in them. Feeling like an old horse dropped off at the glue factory, I faded and was just going through the motions of life.

And the anger. I didn't anticipate the anger aging would provoke. If I had acted on my hostile thoughts, I would have gone to jail or at least picked up trash along the side of the highway. Being unhappy about life was contrary to my nature, and it was disorienting. I was like a butterfly fluttering in a rain storm—and occasionally a hail storm. As I moved into my sixties, I lost myself in all of this.

Work was a distraction that stalled off an impending crash. It was after retirement that my plight coalesced into a funk. Then the rally. A defining moment changed everything. I let down one of the most important persons in my life at a critical time. The unfortunate consequence of that forced me to reframe growing older into something crazy wonderful. This transformation was driven by an awareness of the negative messages I sent to others by how I begrudgingly dealt with the ravages of growing older. I discovered it is important to those who care about me that I be okay. And I was not.

The very thing I dreaded most, being a burden to those I loved, was happening because they worried about me. That was not the person I wanted to be. I longed to give support rather than add to the chaos of their lives. I wanted to matter. So after that defining moment and the enlightenment it delivered, I began to model aging in a more positive light for their sake. This transported me from simply aging well to going *beyond* well, which meant aging in a way that is a gift to others.

After redefining the aging process to mean creating legacy, I reinvented myself as a role model. With a new persona, that of an ancestor, I viewed my life as a gift to my children, grandchildren, and future generations. To be a proper ancestor, it is important that I live life full out to the end.

I came to realize that everything I did, every interaction I had, every expression on my face, every phrase uttered, every word written, every action taken, and every example of resilience makes a difference. How I live matters. My influence flows through generations. As long as I am here, I create legacy, and it can be positive or negative. That is no little thing because legacies are forever.

I also claimed my wisdom. I knew some stuff. I knew not to throw rocks at a skunk. I knew to stay away from people with guns looking for their antidepressants. I knew not to pack vibrating toys in carry-on luggage. I knew that when I said a swear word in front of children, I should not follow up with "Oh shit." And I knew that wisdom is not good for much if it is not shared. So I wrote this book.

At sixty-something I could have one-third of my life left. That is a lot of time to waste. Once wasted, it is time I can't get back, so I broke free of the albatross of aging and embraced the freedom and opportunities that came with it. I moved into a domain rich with possibilities and developed the credo: *This is my time, and it can be my best time.* I got my moxie back, and I'm keeping it forever—no matter what happens.

This book is about how I accomplished that transformation. However, it is not a manifesto on aging, replete with deep philosophical thoughts. It is simply my story, laced with fallibilities and lush with lessons learned from a voyage into the third trimester of life. It is about owning the aging experience. It is about living with purpose. This may sound like an old idea dressed up in new clothes, but this journey bridges the gap between acceptance of life unfolding and having a passion for shaping and sharing it. That is huge. It requires a person to age in a way that enriches the lives of others. It is this passion that compelled me to share my story.

I may be accused of man-bashing while doing so, and for good reason. Over thirty-some years of being single, many a date reminded me of changing my mind about having a baby while in the delivery room. I frequently take pokes at men in this book, in both the career and romance arenas, which is almost more fun than I can stand. But, let me be clear. I love men, and those who bear the burden of being the subject of my humor are adored and memories of them cherished—each and every one. Any bitterness I harbor is directed at sociological circumstances, not at the persons. I hold them blameless— well, mostly. A couple of men were like hugging a cactus, and there was some bad behavior, but I was not an angel either.

Men wrestle with the same dilemmas as women—trying to matter and to find love and companionship in an environment of severe change, biological impulses, and complicated human dynamics. I'm restrained by no inhibitions when portraying that reality, and I make no apologies for my "pokes."

If I could put those men together in a sack, shake them up, and reassemble the pieces, I would have the perfect man or a breathtakingly imperfect one. In a way, I've done that here as a few portrayals are composites of several real characters. Also, names and identifying characteristics have been changed and details tweaked to protect the privacy of others and to make me feel better about my "pokes."

I take plenty of "pokes" at myself as well. After writing an earlier memoir, I felt a sense of relief knowing I would not die with my story still in me. However, the target audience for that book was family, and I held back. This book includes the juicy details left out of that one. Sometimes I do things I shouldn't, and I'm not always a good role model. I can get game-show excited, and I am occasionally obsessive. Because of my audacious nature and extreme irreverence, some of my friends worry that I might write about them—and they should.

Fortunately, most friends are my kind of crazy. I thought about them when I decided what to include and what to leave out. That may get me into some degree of trouble, but I'm up for it. Girlfriends inspired me to be bold so as not to disappoint and quirky so as to entertain. If you find this book amusing, it is because of their influences. If you find it offensive, it is also because of them. (Being vulnerable to the temptations of externalization, I contend that any over-sharing in this memoir is because my spirited friends made me do it.)

If you bought this book seeking a fresh perspective on aging, you will find it. If you enjoy a spunky book with a saucy tone, this book is for you. If you are easily offended, it is not.

When I pick up drafts of manuscripts at a print shop, an ornery fellow who works there surprises me with fake covers such as:

THE TRIALS AND TRIBULATIONS OF
A CROSS-EYED BATON TWIRLER
A story of triumph over adversity.

THE ADVENTURES OF A DISCO CLOGGER
How I Destroyed an Appalachian Moose Lodge.

He takes a risk by doing so. Not all customers have a sense of humor. I am always up for a joke, so I eagerly anticipate his covers. Following his example of courage, I share my sixties experiences. Each person must find their own path. This is mine—how I reframed aging and got my moxie back.

—THE FALL—

WHAT THE HELL HAPPENED?

chapter 1

THE CALIFORNIA CRASH

My moxie got up and went.
Who I was in that moment was a stranger to me.

When I transitioned into my sixties, the naiveté of youth was replaced with the naiveté of age. I was not aging well. Dreams faded, and I was just going through the motions of life. As I grounded myself into my therapist's chair, I was equipped with a comprehensive collection of complaints. Being my usual obsessive self, I would lay it all out there and not leave anything out. I had a list.

"What's up?" Dr. Amy asked.

"I'm no good for anything. My retirement dreams are fading because I can't master the technology required to write. I can't operate a DVD, cell phone, GPS, thermostat, or computerized hot water heater. Using a remote is like flying a space ship. I'm unable to tell the difference between HD and analog, and I don't know what a browser is. A computer technician asked if my cookies were activated. What kind of question is that? I'm terrorized by a modem and a router, and I accidentally take pictures of my feet with my cell phone.

"The television suddenly went to black and white, and I must run to the bedroom TV to find out what color they painted the walls on *The Home and Garden Channel*. I'm dysfunctional—a dinosaur. Technology is abusive and geeks are ruining me financially. Oh, yes, another thing. I lost a good portion of my retirement in the recession."

Dr. Amy started to say something, but there was more, and I could no longer hold it in.

"My stomach sticks out so far that security staff at the airport pat it down and I burned it with my curling iron one fine morning. Doctors are determined to discover my ultimate cause of demise and, in the process, were almost successful at causing it. If I took every test they recommend, I'd die or go broke. I'm terrorized by the warnings on prescriptions, and when I pick up pills at the pharmacy, they are a different shape and color each time. I worry they're male hormones and I'll grow a mustache.

"A Hooters waitress called my boyfriend by name when we went out to dinner. He bought a sports car so small that I asked, 'When does the rest of it come in?' Then he began eating fruit for the first time in his life. Not long after I observed him eating a goddamn banana he ran off with a young woman who had a fondness for jean jackets and Game Boy Advance.

"My next boyfriend took up with a cafeteria cashier thirty years my junior who has an obsession with animal prints and was desperate for a new transmission, a credit card, and school supplies for her children. Then there's Coco, the squirrel I feed, who is eating my patio furniture—another betrayal. I'll never trust love again, and there is no such thing as Karma."

Dr. Amy handed me a tissue and started to speak, but there was no stopping me. I had a list.

"Two grandbabies born a year apart must have multiple surgeries. A baby on morphine is just wrong. My mother is suffering, and suddenly she hates green beans and everything else. I want to save her, and I can't.

"Oklahoma does not love me as much as I love it. People around me are victims of political propaganda, and I don't like some of my friends anymore. Liberals think I'm conservative and conservatives think I'm a liberal, radical, vegan, socialist, lesbian communist. Since when is a moderate an outcast? I'm no good to anyone. I'm tired and angry. I want to kill somebody's cat and take a nap."

My head almost touched my knees as I slumped in the chair. I could hardly breathe. Dr. Amy handed me another tissue and paused thoughtfully before responding to the barrage. We had never met, but I had referred friends and family to her, so she knew of me through others.

She went right to work by suggesting I call a television repairman and that I not kill any cats. She convinced me it was not important in the whole scheme of things to know the difference between HD and analog. And she suggested I do some research on how to divorce a squirrel. This was progress. Dr. Amy didn't fool around.

"What happened that brought you to see me?" she asked. To explain my predicament, I needed her to know how wonderful life had been, so she could understand how it contrasted with my current desperate state. An image of what I believed were the glory days came to mind. The scene was vivid. I was traveling extensively for business while directing a merger team shortly before retirement.

Maxwell, a flaming bellman at a fancy Chicago hotel I frequented, noticed my red heels as I stepped out of a taxi. They were deep red with a patent leather finish. Styled with sleek lines and adorned with sculptured heels in a fashionable height, they looked sensational with my black pantsuit. Maxwell could not contain himself when he spotted them and decided to wrestle me for them. This created a rather amusing tussle in the hotel driveway that spilled into the lobby. His obsession was proof that the shoes were to die for and that I was a trendy fashionista.

Any woman in red heels chased by a uniformed bellman in the Fairmont Hotel lobby in Chicago is brimming with moxie. All my life I had moxie, but in my mid-sixties, I lost it. A couple of years into retirement, I put away the red heels. I was in a slump and wearing them didn't feel right anymore.

I had latched onto a victim mentality—a state incompatible with my nature. It ate at me and produced a self-induced crisis —one that drove me to Dr. Amy. The crisis emerged gradually over a couple of days. I didn't see it coming, but it exploded suddenly, catching me and those close to me by surprise.

* * *

I had travelled from Tulsa, Oklahoma, to Anaheim Hills, California, to help my daughter with a new baby. While there,

I overheard a conversation between her and a friend. The gist of their chat was clear. I was in my sixties, and they felt sorry for me. Their concern catapulted the conversation into tones of dread for their own futures. I heard my daughter say, "I'm sure not looking forward to being sixty." This jolted me.

Without realizing it, I was role modeling what it was like to be sixty-something, and it was not pretty. The message, though unintentional, was powerful. *When you reach sixty, everything is down hill from there.* My daughter's interpretation of my aging experience lingered in my mind for several days. These girls had always looked up to me. Now I was pathetic and creating dread.

Their interpretation was accurate. I was coasting—just going through the motions of life. After I stopped working a few years earlier, I became bitter about post-retirement plans that went awry. This was exacerbated by men who left me for younger women. The frame of mind I adopted in response to these losses was in stark contrast to my previous life when I rolled like thunder. An exceptional career and a blissful sense of fun were what I showed to others. This robust history haunted me, and the contrast with my dispirited current state revealed that everything about me now screamed victim.

My internal dialogue caused the people I cared about to dread their own fate. In the days after I overheard my daughter's conversation, a storm brewed in my head. The fact that I painted an angry cloud over the future of others was abhorrent to me. Shame festered. I tried to act like all was normal, but self-loathing overwhelmed me. My response to this was to run.

The incident that triggered my escape was a minor one. I was impatient with my grandson, and my daughter called me on it. Neither she nor I are much into drama, and under normal circumstances this would have been a non-event. But self-hatred is a powerful stimulant, and it provoked in me an emotional lightening bolt.

Not normally one to be overly sensitive or to run from any situation, I had always been like a self-cleaning oven—a tough person who could hands down deal with any challenge. But this day I ran. Without a word to my daughter, I stomped to my room, booked a flight home to Tulsa, called a cab, packed my bags, and marched my sad, sorry ass out to the curb in front of her California home.

While my daughter—stunned and confused—cried in her bedroom with her new baby and a toddler, I sat on the curb beside my suitcase waiting for a cab. I wanted to turn back, but the momentum of running propelled me onward. I suppressed swirling madness by sobbing with a peculiar combination of control and hysteria. Everything about that moment was strange. I knew I was doing something awful that I could never take back, but I couldn't stop myself.

My reaction was so overreaching that it scared me. Abandoning my daughter at a critical time was unforgivable. A kind of death hung over me as I sat on that curb and grieved the loss of my previous self—the one who would never hurt her in such a way. Who I was in that moment was a stranger to me.

* * *

I've since named this incident The California Crash. The event demanded a label because it was a game changer. My decision to run triggered a series of transforming mental shifts that reshaped my future and that of others.

My daughter didn't deserve the disastrous situation I instigated. We had no history of confrontation, and on the long trip home, I anguished over the fear that our relationship could not recover. My cowardly exit haunted me and amplified looming self-hatred. A sense of failure set in so intensely that it washed away any thoughts of good in me. Despair smoldered. Even my running was an exercise in futility. I was running to nothing. My life was empty.

Soon after I arrived home in Oklahoma, my daughter and I talked by phone. Her mercy demonstrated compassion I thought I didn't deserve, but it was there—solid and true. She said, "I'm okay with your choices, Mom. I just wish you weren't so bitter about them."

Her encouragement propelled me into counseling. Although I believed professional help signaled a deficit or frailty I was unwilling to face, there wasn't much I wouldn't do for my daughter. So off I went to therapy and the process of exploring my demons with Dr. Amy.

I might have endured the mentality I described to Dr. Amy the rest of my life had I not experienced The Crash. I harbored many issues. Each interjected its own dose of complexity and anxiety, but the gnawing hurt of lost love was especially fresh and wounding. Divorced for over thirty years, I had a number of splendid serious and not-so-serious relationships. A few left me damaged, but in the younger years I always rallied. Lost loves in my late fifties, though, inflicted mortal wounds.

A couple of men started with me and worked their way down to desperate women. I felt like a poor, pitiful piece of shit to lose my men to such women. Would I have felt better if the guys had traded up? What if they traded me for a young Barbie named Heather or Brittany with a body that should be illegal and a fondness for teddybears? At least I could have made sense out of their compulsions. However, with Barbies, I would fall into the category of chaperone rather than a poor, pitiful piece of shit. A chaperone? Oh lord. I lie. I'd rather they traded down.

After that, I gave up on love for good. During thirty-five years of being single, too many beginnings and endings had transpired. I could no longer recover, and I became unwilling to give to someone else a part of me that could be broken. I'd rather reupholster a recliner.

Cut loose from my moorings, I was liberated—transformed—and I was done. But *the woman doth protest too much.* I was not done. Around, and around, and around I went. In spite of all my good intentions, for some crazy reason I gave a couple of Oklahoma country boys a twirl. These experiences finished me off just before I headed west to an encounter with The California Crash.

Why did I do it? I wasn't through torturing myself. Raised on a farm in Iowa, I had a weakness for the *I hunts it, I kills it, I eats it* types. Oklahoma offers up a plethora of such men. Many are in various states of adventure and misfortune because they haul refrigerators in the back of pickup trucks, embrace religious and gun-toting fanaticism, or get so high that they wait at a stop sign for it to turn green. The attraction for me was always that I saw something shiny. Oversized belt buckles and chrome-embellished pickup trucks sparkled, and the men did too. But I should have known better. Sharks are shiny.

chapter 2

REDNECK MACHO SHITHEADS

There ain't no way you can love him
more than his dog or his horse does.

On our first date, Dillon exited the Tulsa convenience store exuding easy confidence. He looked ruggedly handsome in Wrangler jeans fitted just right and crumpled a bit at the ankle. Roper boots polished with dirt and a studded leather belt adorned with an oversized, shiny buckle finished the look. He hiked himself easily into the chugging diesel Ford truck. His presence filled the cab with the woody smell of Stetson aftershave.

Dillon placed an empty styrofoam cup stuffed with a napkin in the credenza cup holder—a mystery to me. Spit cups were not in my arsenal of worldly experiences. The mystery unfolded as he opened a can of Skoal, dipped in two fingers, scooped out a wad, tucked the gooey mess in his mouth between teeth and gum and licked his fingers.

Horrified, I said, "I can't believe you're doing that."

"I'm a doin' it."

"But it's gross. It's a non-negotiable for me."

"Well then, darlin', I'll just have to open the door and roll you out into the street."

Be still, my heart.

The message was clear—*if you don't like it, tough.* I looked at Dillon and decided I liked it. I'm a sucker for a man who calls me darlin' even though he is a redneck macho shithead. This label might appear offensive to some, but any man who deserves that designation is proud of it. I use the term affectionately as I have a soft spot for redneck macho shitheads.

Although I'm not the outdoorsy type with a propensity to lean up against a tree in a picture, cowboys grow on me like mold in a bathhouse. Several have complicated and decorated my life. When I pull into a driveway and a skinned deer is hanging from a tree in the front yard, I want to cook a man some biscuits and gravy. Blood dripping onto the grass and herding dogs jumping up trying to get a piece of it enhances the impulse, and I am so-o-o-o in. It is a sickness.

Even though loving such men was a questionable activity, love came in that form, and I went for it. Such choices were equivalent to attaching myself to a rodeo bull, but I frolicked with country boys off and on over the years.

These fellows sucked me into the vortex of the NRA and bail bondsmen and inspired more failed New Year's resolutions than I care to count. Even so, I stayed when I should have said, "I ain't takin' no mo rides on your big green tractor, dickwad."

Several types of country boys populate the country landscape: down to earth farm boys (who give their women rides on their tractors), gentlemen cowboys (who wash their women's cars and gas them up), wild and wooly cowboys (who buy their women trucks), and rednecks (who buy their women guns and ammo). All of them take their women to dinner at Cracker Barrel.

Then there are redneck macho shitheads—reckless, rowdy, real cowboys with redneck tendencies—for whom, unfortunately, I developed an attraction. These guys dream of a license to drive a tank, store tractor parts in the bathtub, and take their women to dinner at Bass Pro shops. Such men are intense, as if coiled like a rattler. The likelihood of a connection with one working out for me was as promising as getting ice cream in the mail.

Several of these fellows chased me hard and scored high in the romance department, although one was incapable of existential sugar. He considered a night out at Lucky's Lizard Lounge a fanciful event, and his lack of finesse in the romance department left me feeling as though I had been felt up by Captain Hook.

In spite of attributes that suggested incompatibilities, I occasionally took a right turn down crazy street toward a redneck macho shithead, and I didn't always signal. These involvements were encouraged by a philosophy I had adopted at that time: People cross your path for a reason. This assumption caused me to relate to a man in the same way I would react to a lost puppy who followed me on a walk. I would take him home, feed him, and play with him until he found his forever home.

* * *

This nonsense took place in the context of Tulsa, which is far enough into the interior of Oklahoma to provide protection from Kansas and Texas. Full of contradictions, the state's southern evangelistic values provided a severe contrast to a divorce rate second only to Nevada and a wild-west, oil-rush mentality.

Oklahoma was, and still is, a place like no other. It was interpreted by me as a wonderland when I moved here in 1966 at the age of twenty-one, an Iowa farm girl out of my element. It was a struggle to adapt initially, but I soon navigated the lifestyle idiosyncrasies. In some respects the Oklahoma culture suited me better than the Iowa one.

Raised on a farm in a small Iowa community, the enforced conformity of the heartland shaped me. With strong northern European influences, no one in Iowa showed emotion over religion or anything else. Strict adherence to societal norms was required. Diversity didn't exist. Stability was valued and rebels denounced. Integrity was compulsory. Adventuresome spirits were stymied and high rollers shunned. At that time, divorce was rare and scandalous. These characteristics contrasted sharply with Oklahoma's wild and rowdy culture.

When I came to Tulsa in the 1960's, it was known as the Oil Capital of the World. Blond, manicured, bejeweled women in Mercedes cruised the streets. A multitude of thriving steak restaurants and private clubs catered to oilmen in starched shirts, seam-pressed Levi jeans, gold

and blazers. Downtown bustled with an
...e of cultural events financed by wealthy oilmen.
... reverberated with lively music venues and
...g clubs. In contrast, Oklahoma was *dry*, and a
...had to fill out forms to get an alcoholic drink.

...oma still suffers from a multiple personality
...der. It's as though *Saturday Night Live's* church lady
...Michael Douglas's greedy character in *Wall Street* had
...by. Then Jed Clampett struck oil.

...the early years, neighboring states nourished a white,
...glo-Saxon, protestant, midwestern culture. Farmers
...ilt white farm houses, large red barns, and a multitude
of sturdy outbuildings while Oklahoma bore the markings
of Indian Territory.

Bleak landscapes peppered with tents, trading posts, and
lean-to houses were populated by Indians, outlaws, and
Civil War refugees. Then the land runs in 1889 introduced
homesteaders. Later the oil boom hit with a fury. That
brought in the railroad, which changed everything.
Neighborhoods of ostentatious mansions sprang up and
Tulsey Town became the city of Tulsa.

Art deco was fashionable during the oil boom, and that
style is broadly reflected in the city's architecture as
opposed to the Federal and European styles popular in
other states. The contrast between the brash oilman
mentality and the evangelistic one was illustrated when
one businessman touted the art deco influences and
another endorsed it by responding, "Jesus loves art deco."

Jesus must have loved oil as well, because the city
thrived. Over time, though, the petroleum industry's
influence faded. Today Oklahoma is more representative

of surrounding states while still maintaining a flavor of the rugged southwest. Composed of a thriving agricultural market, it also harbors enough southern influences to produce a fair representation of redneck macho shitheads who still believe in the beer fairy.

Divorced and on my own in 1975, I raised my children and advanced my career in Tulsa and have long considered myself an Okie. Although I dallied with country boys for several years, I live an urban lifestyle in downtown Tulsa. You could say I'm a metropolitan gal who never quite reached the level of sophistication and refinement that label implies.

* * *

My attraction to country boys stems, no doubt, from being raised on a farm in Iowa. I idolize my dad and brothers, but there is a big difference between an Iowa farm boy and an Oklahoma country boy.

This is because many Oklahoma country boys are cowboys. They're like farm boys on speed. Dating one made me feel like a dog chasing a race car. I couldn't keep up. When he stopped, I didn't know what the hell to do with him. The man was everything I wanted and nothing I needed.

Loving a cowboy is similar to consuming a cinnamon roll made up of half the annual Oklahoma wheat harvest. Still, Oklahoma country boys are, or I should say were, irresistible. What good is self-destructive behavior if you don't destroy yourself? So more than once I wrapped my arms around a honky-tonk man.

Cowboys smell like leather. It's a subtle aroma unless they are wet or gathered en masse, at which point it becomes pungent with musky attributes. At times they smell like a blend of leather, cow shit, hay, and horse hair. That's not attractive, but with rough hands, tanned faces, sturdy demeanor, well-worn boots, and Wranglers fitted just so, the appeal remains.

I awoke one morning from partying the night before to find Dillon and his buddy sprawled on my white, contemporary living room sectional, boots strewn haphazardly on the floor. Cowboy hats shielded manly, sun-weathered faces from the morning sun filtering in through sheer curtains in my downtown Tulsa loft. The juxtaposition was intriguing. To me, they were a vision on the level of Butch Cassidy and The Sundance Kid, at least on the surface.

In my demented state, I concluded I'd died and gone to heaven and proceeded to fry up bacon, eggs, and hash browns. Extra bold coffee brewed as I checked the refrigerator for their brand of beer. It didn't occur to me to acknowledge that this syrupy interpretation of these two wildebeests on my sofa suggested that I had lost my compass. In my mind, they were a gift. It is a sickness.

In contrast to my cosmopolitan digs, Dillon lived on a little piece of heaven in the country (a micro ranch) where ticks and spiders were hell-bent on disturbing my freedom to pursue happiness. His empire included two horses, a herding dog, and enough cattle to avoid the designation of having a big hat and no cattle.

At breakfast, flies dive bombed biscuits and gravy and backstroked in orange juice. Cows bellowed in the pasture —mommas separated from calves or bulls challenging each other. A herding dog growled while frantically attacking a mole hole in the front yard, and a feeding truck tooted in the field of a neighbor's ranch while a herd of cattle chased it looking for their daily allotment of hay.

We sometimes slept out under the stars in the bed of his truck where Dillon dreamed of Montana and I dreamed of him. This sounds romantic, but in addition to the presence of mosquitoes, lying in a sleeping bag with a cowboy was the wrong way to paradise. When his dog, Tango, nosed his way in, I scooted over and hoped the accompanying fleas and ticks had a strong preference for herding dogs.

This situation foretold a problem. In spite of any redeeming qualities a cowboy possesses, he is a fantasy bound to fade because there ain't no way you can love him more than his dog or his horse does.

When Dillon signed up for a new rodeo (some cowboys call relationships rodeos) with a woman thirty years my junior, I was shell shocked. I swore off men, purchased a vibrator, and named it Sam Elliott.

It is not good for any man, redneck or otherwise, to know a woman has a vibrator, let alone that she named it Sam Elliott. Stuart is a better choice. (A woman can defend her decision to name her vibrator by accusing a guy of naming his vacuum cleaner Lulu.)

Men are intensely threatened by vibrators and are driven beyond reason to render them unnecessary. The male's propensity to view every activity as sport and to compete vigorously in any situation can often be played to the female's advantage. Determined to one-up a vibrator, a man will hum if you ask him to—every time, on cue—an audition of sorts.

With Dillon gone, I undertook some masochistic introspection and withdrew from the romance scene. *I am no longer single. No more rodeos for me—ever.*

* * *

So . . . when Tanner sauntered up to me for the first time, looking better than any man has a right to, I was determined that the voice of reason would prevail. It didn't. A heavy-duty presentation of a man, he was a ruggedly handsome fellow with leathery skin, an intoxicating grin, and a gait that reminded me of my father. He pursued me with the persistence of a carnival barker, and I jumped into the lake naked with another cowboy. It is a sickness. A poem reflects my decision.

COWBOY CHARM

I don't like chew.
I don't like you.
I won't ride a horse,
But I will, of course.

Tanner was a linear man, quick to get to the heart of a matter. When confronted with an ink blot, a reclinable seat, or a dance position, he saw something erotic. Three of anything was a mènage á trois. When I suggested dinner at a sushi restaurant named *In the Raw*, he assumed I was going to get naked. He considered *horsefly* a term of endearment, and when I crawled into bed in a sexy teddy, he asked, "Can we lose the jump suit?"

He was also a dancin' fool. The man artfully maneuvered women around a crowded dance floor like a pedigreed cutting horse working cattle. I stuck with him longer than I should have because he did a mean country two-step and a splendid Texas shuffle, which was more fun than anything.

With his hand in mine, he hauled me urgently and directly to the dance floor as soon as we arrived at a dance hall because that was why we were there—not to party, but to dance. There, the magic happened. We became at one with the place. Lights shone mystically through a haze of smoke, music pounded, and shadowy figures hovered throughout.

Country dancing involves dancing in circles like roller skaters. Wild and rambunctious, it bears no resemblance to the ballroom scene. While spinning and twirling, nightclub lights dart by like comets with tails. As the woman, you get thrown around so harshly that you could take off like a frisbee if your partner doesn't hold on to you. This is normally not a problem since the cowboy latches on rather like the birthing ritual of beta fish where the male squeezes the eggs out of the female and sometimes she dies.

Cowboys often don't play well with others, particularly in honky-tonks. They will kick someone's ass at the drop of their summertime straw cowboy hats. "Let's take it outside," they say. Most don't have the self-discipline to take it outside, though. They'll get it on right then and there, and it's not a boxing match. It's a take down.

Although he had a gentle side, Tanner was no exception. A big guy—so tall that he could put things on high shelves just to mess with people—his size alone gave him an advantage in testy situations. I knew he was hankering for a fight one night when he and another fellow stood in a forest of longneck bottles and engaged in a stare down reminiscent of bulls in a pasture. Tanner said, "I came here to drink beer and kick ass, and I'm all out of beer." In that moment I knew I would be washing blood out of his plaid pearl-snap western shirt after exiting the acute care center, that is, if I was not bailing him out of the county jail. Once the buzz wore off, he would be hungry. Like most cowboys, Tanner had a kitchen devoid of food where without me he survived on tater tots.

Cowboys work hard so it is important to nourish them. During roundup, they work daylight to dark. I delivered thermos bottles of coffee to the barn at sunrise as they saddled up. They were uncharacteristically quiet. Sounds were limited to the clinking and clunking of gear and tack and the occasional blubber or stomping of a horse. Silhouettes of cowboys carrying saddles loomed as they strode to their mounts. Dust swirled around them, dancing in the sunlight beaming in from barn doors large enough to accommodate hayracks.

In the evenings Tanner came home tired, bruised, crippled, dirty, reeking of cow shit, and carrying a bag of calf testicles. He relished deep frying them in heavy grease, assigning them exotic names, and feeding them to greenhorns who assumed they were eating something similar to Chicken McNuggets.

Tanner had a severe judgmental mentality and a disturbing set of core values that were difficult to accept, and I eventually tired of them. I vowed to stop punishing myself. I was emphatic. *I am done here. No more. I am no longer single.* And I meant it.

* * *

So . . . as I put on my big girl boots and got back in the game with Cooper, a sweet-talking country boy with a beguiling grin and eyes that twinkled mischievously, I knew I was in over my head. It is a sickness.

Fun broke out wherever Coop went. He had a steady, responsible nature, but he was full of contradictions. An endearing playfulness contrasted glaringly with a reckless, intense nature. Scrappy, reactive, and quick to respond to any sign of disrespect, he settled disputes independently. (Coop was not the type to go to Judge Judy for anything.) His interest in defending my honor was frightening and had me on edge a good part of the time. If he could, he would brand his cows and his women.

Still, his comedic inclinations and sense of fun were a source of amusement. The man could dish it out, and he could take it. His friends relished his rascally exuberance and delighted in his tendency to step into trouble every other step. When he said "Watch this," you were going to see something interesting, if not frightening. A common expression of his was "Whoops," which was foreboding because Coop was a gun guy, and he shot things willy-nilly.

He believed it was okay to shoot a woman if she was stealing his horse because Willie Nelson said so in a song, and he applied similar logic to many things. Holding stubbornly to the cowboy way, he would "cowboy up" and just shoot. The man was capable of shooting a turkey and scaring everyone in the grocery frozen food section.

Cooper had a sign on his front door with a picture of a gun on it that read, "I don't call 911." He shot a dog because it wouldn't come to him when he whistled. A stray dog got shot because it got sprayed by a skunk, not that he wouldn't have shot the dog if it had not been sprayed by a skunk. In contrast, he was solidly bonded to a bi-polar dog so mean that when Coop didn't answer his phone, I worried Brute had eaten him. Dogs fall into distinct categories, and women do so as well. Coop was a hunter, and hunters are complicated like that.

I labeled Coop a free-range cowboy. He could barely tolerate being inside and occupied himself with a series of outdoor activities. He was the inclusive sort when it came to his women and insisted I go quail hunting with him. I protested because I once saw a gun kick so hard it bloodied a lip and chipped a tooth and because Macy's was having a Red Dot shoe sale. No way was I going to go hunting for anything but shoes.

So . . . as I climbed into his 4x4 Ram truck, I was outfitted in camouflage clothes, rubber boots, and an iridescent orange vest because that poetic genius said my blond hair reminded him of waves of grain in a Kansas wheat field. Brute sat between us, his enthusiasm for a ride in the truck creating enough drool to produce a slip and fall.

Noting the full gun rack in the back window and an ample supply of ammunition under foot, I confessed, "You need to know that I suffer from failure to fire in a timely manner."

Undeterred, he responded, "That's okay. You can make yourself useful by flushing out quail. Just run around in the field and yell 'Whoo hoo!' Brute will do the retrieval."

This produced a visual of me running in a zigzag pattern through a field, my wheat-colored hair blowing in the wind, Brute bounding along beside me, Coop blasting away at a covey of quail taking flight, and buckshot raining down.

There's a fine line between hunting and looking stupid. Coop and his buddies hunted coyotes with four wheelers and cell phones, an activity they considered a sport on the cultural level of a fox hunt. I questioned this since the coyotes didn't get to have cell phones, but there is no reasoning with gun and ammo guys.

These macho men hunt deer by sitting in trees where they wait for Bambi to meander by. This can take a while, so they tie themselves to trees to keep from falling out if they doze off. This is done at four in the morning in freezing cold weather. Dressed in clothes suitable for a polar expedition and boots dosed with deer urine, these brave hunters carry guns capable of felling a Canadian moose.

Coop and his buddies bought a portable toilet, painted it in a camouflage pattern, cut windows in it, hauled it into the woods, and sat in it to hunt deer, which proves my point about the fine line between hunting and looking stupid.

Hunting passion runs deep. Coop believed the opening day of deer season was a religious holiday. His spiritual enthusiasm was poignant, and a poem came to mind one day as I prepared rabbit and dumplings:

HUNTER'S FANTASY

See the bunny.
Shoot the bunny.
Eat the bunny.
Make a hat.

See the bunny.
Shoot the bunny.
Eat the bunny.
Make a lucky charm.
I've already got a hat.

Hunting is dangerous, and not just because of guns. Explosives are sometimes required. This is illustrated in a tale about a guy who threw a stick of dynamite onto a pond to break up ice for duck decoys. His new, not-fully-trained bird dog ran out on the ice, picked up the sizzling stick and chased the man around trying to return it. Confused by the man's unusual response to her retrieval, the dog jumped into the cab of his new cherry red, fully-loaded, Super Duty, V-10 Turbo, Ford off-road pickup truck and blew it up. This suggests that a woman who accompanies a hunter could be sitting in his truck chewing on beef jerky, listening to Toby Keith, and all hell breaks loose.

For a romantic weekend, Coop planned a fishing trip, which required putting bait on hooks. I prefer to rescue bait. While it's convenient for a man to pee out of a boat in the middle of a lake, this is not true for a woman. So I was not going to go fishing, and I held that position.

So . . . as I hung my sorry ass over the edge of a fishing boat because Coop said I was prettier than a Minnesota lake, he held on to me so I wouldn't fall in. No cowboy wants to lose his woman in Oologah Lake.

With Coop operating with the enthusiasm of an Apache warrior, I began to feel as disposable as that stray dog sprayed by a skunk. So we broke up.

* * *

In spite of Dr. Amy's counsel and encouragement, I've not found my love bearings again. The prospect sometimes crosses my mind, and I am tempted to revert back to old behaviors and tie a brand new bow around the same old thing. However, I've already had three cowboys too many. When tempted, I remind myself, *I've had this nightmare before, and I was naked.* So I've stopped the "Love a cowboy. Repeat. Repeat. Repeat." If another one shoots me, I hope he kills me because I don't want to suffer. I'd rather be an oil soaked bird. Still, it is a sickness. . .

My romantic experiences were not limited to men with a fondness for camouflage and kick-ass trucks. I was an equal opportunity romantic and mixed it up with a variety of men—some without verbal or physical dexterity, one who amused a cop by tipping a breathalyzer back like a bottle, and several others who were marvelous representations of their gender.

Divorced at thirty, I've been single for over thirty years. Some might find it strange that I never remarried. I confess to harboring an aversion to marriage, but I have no doubt I would have taken the plunge with the right person. I just never found anyone I could envision being with forever.

All those years of relationships wore me down and contributed to my mid-sixties crisis. As I tried to make sense of The California Crash, it became necessary to make peace with the downsides of my romantic history. For that reason, the rough edges of love are focused on here at the expense of the positives. However, even the few bummer relationships that ended poorly had their moments of splendor.

Some wonderful men entered my life, and I was the beneficiary of their exceptional attributes. Each took me on a fantastic adventure. I have no regrets, well, almost none. A person really can have too much fun. I almost hurt myself having fun. Still, a girl can only take so many tattoos on the heart.

chapter 3

DON'T DATE STUPID
(PUN INTENDED)

Love is like falling into a vat of caramel. It is
sweet, messy, and sticky—and it can be annoying.

I once thought a man was mysterious because he was quiet only to discover he was just stupid. My girlfriend argued that he wasn't stupid. "He's just a simple man," she said. I generally placed considerable credence in her opinions. She was exceptionally intuitive and had a reputation as a savvy, no nonsense kind of gal.

When one of her dates groused that he spent forty dollars on her dinner and wouldn't be able to sleep because she wouldn't go to bed with him, she dug two twenty dollar bills and a sleeping pill out of her purse, handed them to him, and told him to get out. She investigated men before going out with them and discovered such things as the requirement to notify people before moving into a new neighborhood. So I generally went with her judgment, but I couldn't accept her theory on this guy. He was a few watts short of a night light. I was sure of it.

Although I was not qualified to question his gene pool, strong evidence supported my premise. This kind of man says such things as "Dogs are used in Afghanistan to sniff out roadside IUDs." (Crotch sniffing hounds, I guess.) Such a fellow could confuse a mortar pool for a motor pool and spend his Vietnam tour hauling a howitzer around in the jungles instead of smoking pot and repairing vehicles in a maintenance garage in Cam Ranh Bay. Ask him what he's up to, and he gives his weight.

What I thought was cool confidence was a state of absolute contentment. His co-workers said they had to stand him up next to a pole to tell if he was moving, and they called him "lightning." We ran into friends one day and one said to him, "I didn't recognize you without your couch." At times, I wondered if I should take his pulse.

His favorite cereal was Lucky Charms and his favorite meal was chips smothered in Velveeta, but he would devour anything. I worried he would eat my potpourri. On Saturday mornings he watched cartoons while I read the paper. He wouldn't use his seat belt because in a wreck he wanted to be "thrown clear." All evidence suggested he suffered from "dain bramage" of some sort. It seemed appropriate that he seek his own level. There must be a woman out there somewhere watching *Spin and Marty*.

I wasn't suggesting he be culled from the herd or that he was necessarily stupid in the IQ sense of the word. (I didn't give him a test or anything.) He was not better or worse than me. We were just different. How he operated in the world implied a severe incompatibility with a high-energy, ambition-obsessed woman. Most importantly, he was *not* mysterious.

* * *

I stayed with another man longer than I should have for many reasons. One was his sense of humor, which made the relationship tolerable. It has been said that if a man has money and looks he can get a second date, but if he has a sense of humor, he can see a woman naked on the first date. That may be true. Humor is a spark.

This guy was entertaining to the nth degree. He talked to himself in an Elmer Fudd voice every morning while shaving and viewed the world in a *Saturday Night Live* kind of way. When the winter Olympics were on, he came through the living room in big strides, sliding his feet across the floor, and swinging his arms broadly.

I had to ask, "What are you doing?"

"Ice skating."

Later I heard thumping on the stairs and again asked,

"What are you doing?"

"The luge," he said.

This went on all day. You should have seen him curling in the kitchen.

This fellow had a habit of asking joggers if they needed a lift. He obsessed about running over pedestrians and speculated about how many extra points he got if he nailed one who was elderly, handicapped, or dyslexic. Anytime he encountered an orb, he suddenly became a fortune teller. He was a hoot. After an archeology field trip, I got this report:

"How was your trip?" I asked.

"Dirty."

"What did you do?"

"Dug in the dirt."

"Did you find anything?"

"Yes! Dirt."

His wit made everything sharper; however, it couldn't outweigh other qualities. Like so many relationships, this one started on a high and faded into indifference. The guy eased into depression and became the omnipresence. His humor took on the sharp edge of dark sarcasm as his disposition declined, but I hung on. Finally, he found someone else more like him. No doubt she made him feel good—better than I did—and I was glad.

* * *

My way in the world of romance reflected significant doses of stupidity. I picked men who demonstrated a remarkable lack of ambition and built fantasies around them. I imagined in them qualities that were not there. It is unreasonable to attribute to an ordinary man the degree of admiration deserved by someone who invented the polio vaccine. Worshiping men promoted unreasonable expectations that sabotaged relationships. This wasn't the guys' fault. It was mine.

I once found a man appealing because I thought the way he squinted from smoke swirling up from a cigarette dangling from the corner of his mouth was attractive. I gravitated to men who stored ammunition under my bed. I had a knack for locating misplaced truck keys, dog leashes, a canister of shotgun shells, or a remote. This attracted a certain kind of man who caused me to wonder who died and left me in charge of dog leashes and ammunition.

One man swept the crazy under the rug until he hooked me in and then emerged as Jack Torrance in *The Shining.* I was lucky to survive. There were red flags, and I should have realized early on that he belonged in a therapeutic asylum setting.

Dating was further complicated by my seasonal affective disorder, which causes me to be comfortable with buying my own Valentine candy. I am content to ring in the New Year, go to movies, and eat in restaurants alone. I make friends that way. When I ask for a table for one, I say to the person seating me, "I have no friends." That person almost always offers to be my friend.

Fiercely independent, I often felt kidnapped when coupled up, and I was not one to fall in love with my kidnapper. Relations were further complicated by an uncontrollable desire to make the home a warm and comfortable environment for my mate. Therefore, I over-functioned. The compulsion to rescue men from chicken flavored ramen noodles is powerful.

This is a problem because most men have a propensity to believe home is a hotel, and the house quickly becomes their environment. I'm in the kitchen peeling potatoes and smashing garlic cloves while a brooding man reclines on my couch with his feet on the coffee table. A dog sits in my spot adoring him.

At one with the remote, the man enjoys an action movie or music that is just noise. Surround sound blasts forth while I hover over the kitchen sink and wonder what the hell happened to the Bonnie Raitt music I used to play while preparing a bowl of cereal for my supper.

It is not necessary for me to make such sacrifices. Pleasing a man is not that complicated. You just have to get naked and bring beer. Most men are happily blurred, and they can settle in nicely anywhere. As for feeding them, all you have to do is fry something. Ask him if he likes it, and he says, "I ate it." Men will eat anything. I left a pecan pie on the counter, and a guy ate it and had a diabetic incident.

Taking on the role of caretaker and nurturer is risky. Compelled to be bad boys, some men force their women into parental roles. The way to avoid this is to not care if he gets a DUI or if his un-neutered dog gives the house an extreme makeover when the mongrel is left home alone. With such a man, I had no alternative but to take on the mommy role. This didn't end well. Because I wrestled away the keys after his whiskey binges, he found a woman who thought he was God and who got drunker than he did.

* * *

After several unfortunate relationships. I put some thought into what qualities I wanted in a man. I even made a list. (I'm not obsessive.) To dampen my propensity to be attracted to gloomy men, I put shiny sparkly eyes at the top and called my quest for such a man *In Search of Sparky*. Loyalty was the second quality on the list. Fun was third.

Near the bottom of the list at number twenty-three was sex. A girlfriend convinced me to move it up to twelve. Then my rebound man materialized, a ruggedly handsome fellow with shiny, sparkly eyes. Postured to put a tattoo on my heart, *Sparky* projected a manly appeal that induced me to move sex up to number three.

He had lost his woman, and I had lost my man. As wounded lovers, he and I built a transitional relationship on rescuing each other. We helped each other heal and proved there is no such thing as a free rescue. Once we were past the rescue stage, he found another woman to save who made him feel better than I did, and he transitioned again. Not having the courage to tell me (because he was a sensitive guy, not because he was hard hearted), he did what men often do. He grew a scraggly beard and shut down, forcing me to break up with him. He was then free to be her hero.

I would have been better served if I had avoided *Sparky* and gone with a man who thought he was interesting because he collected salt and pepper shakers. The relationship left me feeling foolish. I wanted to believe someone could put all my broken pieces back together. He did that, and then he broke me again.

* * *

Men were a lot of trouble—throwing a dead coyote in my trunk, tracking manure onto the floor mat, leaking oil in my driveway, or leaving a cup of chew in the car drink holder —but they were very much into rescue. I've always been able to take care of myself financially, but I have needed emotional rescue at times.

When newly divorced—before I hit my stride and found my independent nature—I was one of those women whom men could take care of. I got hammered one day after work (in the pre-cellphone era) and rang up my boyfriend, Ronnie, from a phone booth outside a bar. He was a consummate rescuer who put me back together after a jarring divorce, and I knew he would come through.

"Hi! Ronnie, would you come get me? I'm snockered," (Snockered is a term I made up to describe my condition after three drinks and before throwing up.)

"Sure, darlin'. Where are you?"

"I'm not sure. I'm at some bar downtown."

"You stupid bitch. You don't know where you are? How can I come get you if I don't know where you are?"

"I'm thorry, I don't know where I are. I told you I'm snockered. And by the way, Ronnie, you can call me anything you want, but don't you call me thupid."

"You stupid bitch." In his defense, understand that Ronnie meant the "b" word affectionately since he was one of the noble redneck macho shithead breed.

"Ronnie, you can call me anything you want, but don't you call me thupid."

"Shit. Look around for a street sign."

"Okay . . . Honey, I'm at the corner of 'Walk' and 'Don't walk.'"

"You stupid bitch."

"Ronnie, I told you, you can call me anything you want, but don't you call me thupid."

Although I exercised poor judgment by partying without eating, I knew I was not stupid. Ronnie rescued me, as he usually did. I could count on him. I always felt as though he had his hand on the small of my back, gently pushing me forward and ready to catch me if I fell. He may be the only man who loved me completely, and I loved him wholly. Because of that, after five years we gracefully let go of each other, thereby eliminating tormenting incompatibilities. When we broke up, this strong rock of a man shook in my arms. The vulnerability revealed in that moment touched me deeply. No one else ever loved me like that. It was a big love.

I was weak when he found me and strong when he went away. Over time, as I became stronger and fiercely independent, there wasn't much opportunity for him to save me. A strong woman is hard on a man. He could no longer rescue, and that didn't make him feel good.

I didn't make another boyfriend feel good when I had a flat tire on an expressway, caught a ride to a car dealership, and bought a new car. The dealer retrieved mine from the expressway for trade in. When I told my boyfriend I'd bought a new car, he asked, "Why?" Like I had to have a reason. I answered, "Because I had a flat tire."

After overcoming his surprise, he asked guy questions: "What's under the hood?" (Like what was under the hood was important.) "What about the transmission?" (Like I knew anything about that.) I responded, "I have no idea, but the car is white-on-white with leather seats, chrome wheels, an awesome stereo, a makeup mirror that lights up, and it goes down the road. I know, because I test drove it."

He chastised me for not investigating the engine and transmission, and he determined I had done a bad thing— and that I was stupid. That was one of several reasons why he is no longer my boyfriend.

I'm not suggesting that the mechanics of a car are not important, or that I am not off the charts impulsive at times, or that it is not important to be inclusive when it comes to boyfriends, but this was a man who had the potential to convince me to buy a truck.

He also had his own impulse issues. He occasionally drank so much that he drove down both sides of the road at the same time. He routinely got sunburns so bad he looked like someone had dipped him in cherry juice, and his tools were cleaner than his silverware. He had virtues, though. He was steady, he had a good heart, and he loved me. He deserved a chance to participate in picking out a car for his girlfriend, and he didn't get it.

A man feels good when rescuing—temporarily anyway. Conversely, he feels inadequate when rescued. I used to be a consummate rescuer as well as the asshole whisperer, so I was a soft place to land for several men. This invited a curse that put out the flame eventually. It is best if both partners come together from positions of strength.

* * *

The quality of eligible men declines as one gets older. This makes it tempting to settle and date down, which is stupid. Who wants a guy who attempts to order nachos in a French restaurant or who eats inferno chimichangas on a date causing you to wonder who farted? I introduced a man to brie, and he hooked up with a bartender with rented furniture. This was a tad hurtful, but knowing the person you take up with might be the person you become, I viewed the failed relationship as a near miss.

Those who drink a lot are not a good match for me. Given my tendency to get snockered (throw up) after three drinks, I had no desire to take up with a man who goes to the liquor store each morning for breakfast. Getting the keys away from a guy like that is like prying a ball from the mouth of an ill-trained, overly enthusiastic Golden Retriever. These are men who are drunk when you break up with them so you have to do it again the next day.

Younger men are not a good bet either, unless you're looking for someone to raise. Orphans seeking adoption, they chase older women like Pac Man eating up dots. Going out to dinner, though, means you will eat jalapeño poppers at Sonic. Later you have great sex on a futon.

The youngsters only play. They don't stay. There are just too many incompatibilities. When I was in my thirties, younger men I dated were still paying off student loans and living in an apartment with four or five buddies and a pitbull or in Mom's basement with a pitbull. Now, younger men are in their fifties, and they don't yet relate to the need to stir powder into morning coffee, to conceal back fat, or to microwave bubblegum so it doesn't pull out bridgework. When a relationship with a younger man is over, you leave him a better man, and you're left to wonder what the hell just happened.

It's best to stick to your age group, but it's difficult for women in their sixties to attract sharp men. Those men can land younger women, so they do. Opportunistic losers are abundant, though. A woman can go out on Friday night and have a boyfriend Saturday morning, but the best thing to be said about him might be that he is optimistic about improving his credit rating. Perhaps his occupation is waiting for his next court appearance, or the only thing to sleep on in his apartment is a blow-up doll.

* * *

Even a thoughtful man can be amazingly insensitive. It's irritating to be in a bad mood and your man doesn't notice. I overlooked a lot and was generally overly accommodating in relationships. I would celebrate an anniversary dinner in a Bass Pro shop without complaint. I was gracious when my guy wanted to watch an action movie and I wanted to watch a chick flick. We compromised and watched an action movie. We may even have watched it and a sports event at the same time, switching back and forth. (Nothing is more tedious than a man with a remote.)

Most of the time when I was coupled up, we lived in the man's world, and I was just visiting. It was not uncommon for my man to expect me to watch him play sports although there was no way he would watch me do anything except undress. I visited his family and accepted his flawed friends while he dished out harsh judgments and made fun of mine. I endured his television shows while he would not tolerate mine. And I had to listen to his music. (If I hear Free Bird on surround sound one more time, I'll go insane.) Only begrudgingly would he ever listen to mine.

* * *

At several points in my many years of being single, I swore off men. Single people do that a lot, both men and women. When I did so in my early sixties, I operated from the perspective that *men don't like me*. Although this was an inaccurate interpretation, it served the purpose of preventing me from dating stupid. In spite of this negative attitude, I got asked out. The scenario usually went something like this:

"Would you like to go to dinner sometime?"

"You are very brave to ask, but no thank you."

"Why is that brave?"

"Because men don't like me."

"But I like you."

"No, you don't."

"Yes, I do. I like you."

"No you don't."

"Yes, I do. I really do. I like you a lot."

"Well, you would get over that."

What led to this frame of mind was men who stormed into and out of my life like tornadoes leaving me ravaged. After many years of wonderful relationships, I was in my late fifties when I experienced betrayals for the first time. My men found distressed, substantially younger women who provided the pulsating life force they required to feel virile and enough calamity to allow them to be heroes.

Some women would have fought for their men. I didn't. Betrayal was a deal breaker. When I discovered a man was interested in another woman, I gave him to her as a present, and I never regretted that decision. Some would call this revenge. I call it the hug of acceptance.

* * *

In spite of bad choices (the *I don't care what everyone else says, I like you anyway* decisions), I never completely gave up on love. Men in uniform were appealing. UPS delivery men caught my eye. Guys in cable company shirts were strangely captivating as well as mall security guards. However, these men were trouble waiting to happen. To avoid taking the bait and dating stupid, I dreamed of Gene Hackman—the unattainable who wouldn't disappoint and leave me shattered and craving more.

Such attractions were disturbing, but even worse, I found pirates appealing. The sheer desperation of that shook me to the core. A girlfriend invited me to a costume party, and I worried pirates might be there or, worse yet, a robot. I've had a thing for mechanical men since I got engaged to a bomb squad robot at a Marine base in San Diego. If there was a robot at the party, I would no doubt say to him, "Oh, there you are. I've been looking for you all my life."

These love issues set the stage for The Crash. I no longer looked at an attractive man and thought, *Mmmm. I want some of that.* Instead, I felt like a cat about to be hit by a car. Love fell off the radar, but it is an opiate and it smoldered there. Flow with me here. It gets worse.

chapter 4

ONLINE DATING MADNESS

*People who lie on the Internet
complain that people lie on the Internet.*

Oklahoma prospects looked good when I explored finding love online. Photoshopping had been invented, and I could handle a lawn mower. Nothing is more attractive to an Okie man than a woman who mows, and there is never a car too fast, a truck too jacked up, or a woman too pretty. Then there is perfume that smells like bacon.

I resorted to this desperate digital age measure because love is a stubborn intruder. Although I preferred an arrangement where I connected with men by my people contacting his people, an intervention of sorts, I had no people. So I got stupid and went online. This required a shift in core assumptions, but I became convinced it could work when my boyfriend found a girlfriend that way.

I discovered him in our unlit office late at night, the glow of the screen revealing intense concentration. The intermittent pace of keyboard pecking and staccato-like noise reminiscent of mice scampering in an attic suggested chat room action. His expression disclosed the ardent, leering sentiment of desperate lust. I stood unnoticed in the shadows, digesting what this meant and then, not wanting to believe what it meant, I meandered back to bed. *This too shall pass.* It didn't. Soon thereafter, he confessed that he wanted to meet his chat room pal and asked my permission to do so. I told him to get out.

Since, the Internet was very, very good to him, I thought I would give it a try. In retrospect, I realize I should have drawn the same conclusion about dating sites that I drew when spotting a plunger beside a toilet. It is possible to get a good outcome, but the odds aren't good.

When I checked out the dating site profiles of the sixties crop of old men with pot bellies, comb-overs, and gray beards, I discovered they preferred women who were *fit, toned, and athletic.* To get *the body,* these men were willing to put up with a lot: floral decor, stuffed animals, and someone waking them up in the middle of the night to ask, "Where is our relationship headed?"

Occasionally a man "winked" at me (an online flirting process equivalent to a stare across a crowded barroom). This happened because they were really, really old and to them I was a younger woman and because I lied by omission. I didn't admit in my profile that I was *soft, ripply, and sedentary* with breasts that resembled tube socks filled with sand. I left no clue that I wore orthopedic inserts or that I'd graduated to elastic waistbands. And there was no need to reveal that my butt felt like cottage cheese. My omissions made me nervous about meeting someone in person. The man would expect the woman in my photoshopped picture, and I would show up. So I never had the courage to meet anyone, but I did chat with a few.

In response to old men who sought a woman who was *fit, toned, and athletic*, I had some fun and said on my profile that I preferred someone built like George Strait, who walked like Richard Gere, sang like Michael Bublé, had the stamina of Sting, and was into nude hang gliding and making me breakfast. I got some nibbles. I suspect the nude hang gliding thing did the trick.

I believe some men were having fun with the online dating process as well. A philosophical intellectual asked me, "What happens to the hole when the cheese is gone?" I replied, "You are so deep." A comic book collector sprinkled his emails with *Shazam! Biff! Bam!* and *Boom!* Other men concocted names fashioned after animals, things of nature, or verbs. A guy named Thor winked at me, which was disconcerting. Then there was Skillet. Really?

One fellow, who lived in the realm of irrelevance, asked for my sign. Not much into such fanciful things as astrology, I was tempted to have some fun and say "Feces." However, this sign could appeal to a perverted base of the male population, which was a tad scary. So I said my sign was "Asparagus."

The mental strain of online dating was obvious. Some men communicated with so many women that they couldn't remember who they told what. One fellow's emails sometimes stopped mid-sentence as though he'd lost his train of thought. Another occasionally communicated with one word sentences, such as "Well" or "Gee." That was it. The end. I didn't know how to respond, so I said, "Ditto."

An arrogant fellow with an unscientific belief system assumed mine was the same, which this type of person is prone to do. It is not possible to reason with those who embrace the unreasonable. He had the answers to all the mysteries of the universe. Since I knew no one died and left him in charge of the universe, I disagreed with him on something. He said, "Being smart enough to be a C.P.A., you should know better." *Oh, I know better all right.* The last words this pompous ass heard were, "I think you just called me stupid. You can call me anything you want, but you cannot call me stupid." Shazam! Biff! Bam! Boom!

Another man razzle-dazzled me with this comment, "When you get there, you find there is no there." Unless he was putting me on, this suggested he was in the victim mode, which is not a happy place. I wasn't up for being his sunshine. You only have to make that mistake five times.

An owlish scholar bragged that he was ambulatory. I suspect that anyone who describes himself as ambulatory expects not to be ambulatory soon. A partner who cannot get around on his own does have some appeal. I appreciate opportunities to pre-board in the throes of the airline caste system. However, he also bragged about his financial condition, which meant he owed money to the IRS for back taxes and to a Mercedes financial institution.

The next fellow I chatted up was so Irish that I knew if he hung around very long I'd want him to go be Irish someplace else. Another was into contra dancing, which may be a Cuban revolutionary movement. I also passed on a fellow whose online name was "Gameboy" and another named "Keg Boy." Men in their sixties should have moved out of the frat mode years ago. Then there was the fellow who preferred a woman in the age range of 18-120. I suspected he was not discriminatory. I prefer a man who is selective in order to reduce the odds of catching something.

A man sent me an email in Spanish. I knew no Spanish except what I learned from a Ricky Martin song and what a guy taught me years ago before I made a trip to Mexico. He described it as a friendly, welcoming phrase. Turns out I was saying "Don't fuck with me, buddy," which I realized was not a welcoming phrase when my driver and a hotel clerk did not take to it. This experience left me with some skepticism when a man at the office greeted me in a meeting with some Spanish lingo. I turned to the human resources guy and said, "I want to file a complaint." He asked why, and I said, "I don't know what he said, but I'm certain it was inappropriate." I'm not comfortable with communicating in Spanish when I don't know any Spanish. I mean, I thought quesadilla meant to have a good day and that there was a city called San Joe Za. Perhaps I'm over-thinking this.

* * *

Not all is good on the Internet. My girlfriends call online interactions drive-by-dating—worse than meeting in bars— so they were sympathetic to my misadventures. They shared their experiences:

"When he learned I was a school principal, he wanted to know if I would spank him."

"The guy clearly wanted to ride the goat before killing it."

"He was determined to die of acute debauchery and take as many people with him as possible."

"He put me to bed drunk, and I woke up the next morning in a camouflage NRA t-shirt."

Finally, one friend clicked with an acceptable boyfriend online. The only problem was he had an astounding comb-over. His hair spread across his bald spot like strings on a melon. To convince him to stop the madness, she threatened to adopt a permed, blue-haired, helmet-head style for herself. He stuck to his comb-over, though, failing to realize that bald can be beautiful, or at least better than a comb-over. Anything is better than a comb-over.

Eventually, he grew a beard (a typical male act of rebellion). As a Civil War general look emerged, she went back to the Internet where she met a man from out of town. She picked him up at the airport for their first date and brought him to happy hour with our social group.

He didn't have a comb-over or a beard, so he looked good at first blush. However, a smile revealed that his two front eye teeth were missing. Gone. This predicament would be understandable if it were a temporary state. People in my age group grew up without fluoride, and it's not unusual for us to carry our teeth around in a pocket or purse for one reason or another, but only temporarily. And, we would probably not go on a first date with two missing front teeth. When he smiled, we laughed. I mean, you had to laugh. He was a cheery fellow so he smiled a lot, and when he did, we laughed, and when we laughed, he laughed. Then we laughed some more, and then . . . well, you get the picture.

These situations show how unreliable Internet information can be. Integrity is scarce. Those who pontificate about financial security are on the brink of a financial crisis. People projecting physical vitality are on the cusp of a health crisis. Women who say they are 36-D are really 34-Long. Women lie about their weight and age. Men lie about their height and whether they smoke. People lie with outdated or photoshopped photos. People lie by omission. People lie by exaggeration. People lie outright. People who lie on the Internet complain that people lie on the Internet.

Chasing a man by putting ourselves on the Internet is awkward for women of my generation. We prefer to be chased in person by a man with self-confidence—one who knows what he wants and goes after it. Men are appealing when they are self-assured. I had a boyfriend once (it could happen) who left me alone in a club while he went on a quest for beer. A man passing by began chatting me up. When my boyfriend returned, the man said to him:

"You shouldn't leave her alone. She might run off with someone else."

My boyfriend said, "No, she won't," which was why he was my boyfriend.

* * *

I ruled out men online who listed technology-related jobs on their profiles because the personality type that gravitates to that profession signals the likelihood of a basic incompatibility. I took up with a high-tech guy once who perhaps loved his hardware and software more than me. At his company Christmas party, we sat at a table in a far corner from the action with men who say, "I'm from tech support and I'm here to make you feel stupid."

These techies spoke in acronyms and rehashed fascinating computer events throughout dinner while their women rarely spoke. Much of the conversation revolved around

Oliver, the company's captivating mainframe. Oliver was their idol. An intriguing character in their minds, he would be voted Most Valuable Player in a sports scenario, the Top Avenging Crusader in a video game, or Miss Congeniality in a beauty contest. I don't typically try to change my men's behavior. Instead, I focus on controlling my own, so on the way home I advised my date of my position. "I'm not going to any more of your company parties."

"Why not?" he asked.

"It wasn't fun."

"I thought we had a good time."

"Well, I didn't. We didn't even dance."

"People were dancing?"

I eventually came to terms with the reality that I'm incompatible with men with analytical minds capable of hacking my computer and my heart. When he moved the icons around on my computer just to mess with me, I gave him the boot and distracted myself with a fascination with pirates. I don't think pirates poke around on computers.

Over-sensitized to red flags at this point, I saw them everywhere and rejected every man I came across online or otherwise. There was always something worrisome, little things such as lava lamps, metal detectors, or Elvis paraphernalia. Again, I decided: *I am no longer single.*

* * *

So . . . as I once more signed on to an online dating site, I hoped to find a man who aspired to achieve a higher level of understanding of the female sensibilities and who would make me supper. I dreamed of a back massage that lasted longer than two minutes and a man who knew my whole body like a map—not just the key parts. I fancied a lover who wouldn't toss me over for the remote just because a NASCAR race was starting.

I wanted a man who looked at me the way I looked at bacon, one who wouldn't scare small children or insist on wearing a cowboy hat to a Florida wedding. I accepted that I would never find one who wiped off the counters after washing dishes, and there is no way a man would scrape concrete off a casserole dish or sweep the kitchen floor. I was willing to settle, though, for one who didn't cut the sleeves out of his shirt, didn't interpret housework as cleaning out the garage, didn't install surround sound in my home, and who didn't have a turkey who attacked me when I got out of my car.

Too many of these online prospects in Oklahoma had enough hair on their faces to qualify as chia pets. I don't hate beards if they are nicely trimmed, but in spite of noble efforts, few men can pull one off. Also, I've learned that a beard is often a sign of rebellion, which is a complicated, disturbing condition that causes men to sour and behave like Zulu tribesmen. A beard may also suggest that if a man loans you a book, it will smell like smoke, and if you pat him on the back, pollen and dust will float around and set off an allergy attack.

Often a background of sports paraphernalia reminiscent of a locker room was visible in online photos. Not much into sports, I once asked how many innings there were in a football game. To me March Madness was a sale at Macy's, the Stanley Cup a sailing trophy, and a GI Series a ballgame between soldiers.

Some men posted pictures of themselves relaxing in recliners also occupied by large dogs. Such men proudly displayed dead animals and fish. A lifeless deer splayed out on the tailgate of a four-wheel-drive pickup truck with two-tier gun rack, steel step sides, and what was surely a grinding diesel engine revved up, rockin' and ready to roll didn't do it for me. You gotta know that such trucks smell like cigarettes, manure, and sweat socks.

Men displaying guns looked like they might explode at any minute like a blender without a lid. Such men express affection with the finesse of Sasquatch and consider a chainsaw or an ID etching system an appropriate gift for their woman's birthday. The lack of sensitivity to the female persuasion reflected in their online posts is equivalent to my trying to attract a man by posting that I once sold a breast pump at a garage sale.

These men are everywhere in Oklahoma, and they have the potential to mutate and jump species. Soon the world will be full of them. Such online options caused me to re-think my position: *I am no longer single.*

* * *

So . . . as I signed up with a dating agency in Chicago where I spent much of my time directing a company merger, I hoped to find a more sophisticated man. I was in my early sixties and looking for one five years younger or older than myself. Once I hit sixty, though, finding a quality man became a challenge—something like searching for a palm tree in Detroit.

The agency set me up with men in their seventies and eighties—ten to twenty years older—because to those men, I was a younger woman. The situation was worrisome. They were nice old fellows, and I didn't want to hurt them. I protested to the agency staff who admitted that high-quality men in their sixties preferred younger women. The message was clear. I got it. After that, it became a monumental challenge for any man to convince me he would not leave me for a nymphet if the opportunity presented itself. This intensified my inability to trust, which became the primary issue in my portfolio of emotional hangups.

Men my age who've been stung by younger women may seek a more mature one. However, having hooked up with a young girl requiring rescue, they are left with relationship residue: alimony, a toddler, child support until they die, and a psycho ex-wife on the corner of Prozac and Ambien. (A woman who marries a man significantly older than herself suggests an opportunistic nature or a mental lapse.)

Men's inclination to desire a younger woman is equivalent to my dating the kid who hands me food at the take-out window or the one who changes my oil at Jiffy Lube, which is ridiculous. For old men, a similar prospect is normal and often achievable. Some are waiting for the next crop to turn eighteen. When I was sixty, I went out with a sixty-one year old man who told the friend who introduced us that I was too old for him. He was a leathery old fellow who looked older than I did, so I found his conclusion offensive. Rather than deal with this ridiculous dynamic, I preferred to stay home alone and build couch cushion tents. I concluded: *I am no longer single.*

* * *

So . . . as I entered the single marketplace again, I gave Tulsa boys another try. I focused on the pillar of the community types who wear Brooks Brothers suits, who talk in elaborate detail about the attributes of wine (wine tastes like wine, for god's sake), and who order their salad with dressing on the side. You can find these men online.

The fact that I occasionally swear complicated this strategy. I tried to convince right and proper fellows that I was simply using sentence enhancers, but no matter how I labeled swearing, such men were traumatized when I swore. And I *was* going to swear. I tested their tolerance early on in online discussions so as not to waste time.

An upstanding lawyer asked, "It's a beautiful day. Would you like to hop on the old Harley for a ride?"

"I can't. The people who live in my attic disabled my remote and ate my last PayDay candy bar. Shit, I'm so mad I could kill somebody's cat. Do you have a cat?"

"Did you say shit?" he asked.

"Let me be clear, I said SHIT."

"I'm shocked."

"Well, holy shit."

Although he was so shocked at my language that he failed to react to the prospect of me killing a cat, running one of those stuffy fellows off is not as easy as one might think. In a perverse way my sinful sentence enhancers intensified his interest. As long as he kept me away from his family, neighbors, the bar association, his insurance agent, church folks, minister, choir director, and pharmacist, he could deal with it. Soccer buddies, biker pals, and frat brothers were a different story, though. "How about taking a ride in my Corvette, then?"

"No, thank you. You are very brave to ask, after my swearing and all, but I've got to water my crops on FarmVille. I'm into farming online since Reggie went to jail. Have you ever heard of virtual weed?"

That should do it, I thought. It did. Given my irreverent inclinations, it is not difficult to conclude that I'm incompatible with the uptight, pillar of the community types. Measuring up to standards I didn't embrace was pressure I didn't need. I just wasn't feeling it. Bottom line, if a swear word offended some man I dated, he needed to get a new goddamn girlfriend.

I'm not entirely okay with my swearing. I waver. At times, I wish I didn't say bad words. Other times, like when my foam rubber shoulder pad fell out on the floor in front of my date, I know without a doubt that "holy shit" is the only way to describe that.

There is something natural about swearing. It must be an innate inclination because so many people do it. Little children do it. I was playing with my grandson when my butt accidentally sat on his railroad track. He said, "*Dame* it woman." (sp. intended). I don't know where he got that. I say a lot of bad words, but not those. I don't believe his father ever said them, but he heard them somewhere, and they stuck in his little brain. He had to—had to—use them because they expressed exactly how he felt.

When my tiny, sweet little granddaughter was learning to speak, her mother encouraged her to say "drink."

She said, "Shit."

"No, it's drink," Mommy said.

She said, "Shit."

"Drink."

"Shit."

Finally, Mommy said, "Never mind."

She said, "Neber mine," reached for her drink and said, "Shit."

I'm sorry, but that is a girl after my own heart.

* * *

With the elimination of the righteous, pillar of the community fellows who do not measure up to my low standards, the men attracted to younger women, and the hay baler types who dream of a profession as a fishing guide, few options were left. Odds were, love would not happen for me again. Awareness of this occurred not long before my breakdown in California. It introduced a void and a sense of bleak aloneness. Giving up on love was by choice, but it was still a loss—one that left a gaping hole in my psyche. A raw, naked aloneness set in.

This loss of romantic prospects molded me into a hard, bitter, disappointed woman, and it fed my melancholy. Disillusionment took some of the softness out of me. I had been single a long time. It was grand. It was fun. It was glorious, but it was too much, and it was over. An emptiness taunted me as I concluded: *Love doesn't matter.* It does matter, though. It matters a lot.

chapter 5

TOOLBOXES

You ain't seen crazy yet.

Years ago, Connie and I carpooled downtown every day with other accountants. They were unworldly married men. We were seasoned divorcées. Their curiosity about the world we lived in had no bounds. Being divorced and single was not nearly as fascinating as they imagined, but because it was outside their scope of experience, they were intrigued. So we terrorized them.

One of the ways we did this was to flip out over pickup trucks with tool boxes tucked in their beds. Such vehicles were parked outside a bar we passed on the way home. Connie and I speculated about the owners. We staked claims on men based on which truck we fancied. As we had our party in the back seat, Wall Street Journal conversations came to a halt. The men were captivated. I think they knew we were funning them, but who knows. Right and proper married accountants can only wonder about things outside their sphere of life. Never having had a wife, we girls could only wonder about their world.

Their neatly manicured yards and perfectly balanced landscapes hinted at a polite and conventional lifestyle. Surely, when they got home, a pleasant, accommodating woman in Laura Ashley clothes, who managed a well-kept house and nurtured children, greeted them with dinner.

No doubt these accountants had a toolbox in their garage with a comprehensive set of tools lined up neatly inside. Most likely, a pegboard on the garage wall embellished with tools presented a logical arrangement. Nuts, bolts, screws, and nails were surely organized in designated slots. But none of them had a truck with a toolbox loaded with partially rusted, beat-up tools scrambled helter-skelter in a mix of twine, empty cigarette packages, dirt, gravel, disintegrating hardware store receipts, and ammunition. The fact that Connie and I were fascinated by men with such a setup was an absorbing mystery to our carpool pals.

Although we were putting the guys on, there was something appealing about a man with a toolbox in his truck. I never went into the bar we passed every day, but I dated a few men with such toolboxes. I even gave a boyfriend a toolbox and tools for Christmas. He spent a good part of the day in the garage worshiping them. The guy had a habit of abandoning tools throughout the house. A drill charged in my kitchen. Pliers, wrenches, and screw drivers were scattered throughout the house. I rebelled. When this didn't work, I put makeup in his toolbox.

I imagined him staring at it when he first noticed, puzzled beyond belief, just as I was when I spotted a hacksaw on the coffee table. If I had not done what I did, tools would have no doubt taken up permanent residence in my house. No amount of nagging would have prevented their presence because he saw nothing wrong with it. With my makeup in his territory, he figured out what was wrong with it, and a method of communication was established.

A ladder leaned up against the dining room wall for weeks, so I put a silk flower arrangement on his tool table and applied cupcake stickers to the pegboard. Shortly after, he meandered through the house looking for the source of the problem and corrected it.

When he discovered hot pink floral curtains on the garage window, he knew that taking a chainsaw to my crepe myrtle was not a good idea. This non-confrontational form of retaliation worked better than drama or nagging. It was a mature solution. If my guy complained about my stuff in his territory, I just said, "You started it."

Some days later I opened my panty drawer and discovered a hammer nestled there. I knew instantly I had unknowingly provoked a retaliatory act. Off I went to the garage where I discovered my sunscreen on his tool table. Damn. I started to feel bad, but instead I celebrated that we were communicating. It's good to communicate.

* * *

Toolboxes have a mystical appeal. They are an extension of a man and, like a vehicle, reflect the personality of the owner. So as I emptied out a house after a breakup, I stared at the guy's toolbox, which he had left behind, and contemplated what to do with it. I felt a sense of reverence about it, almost as though it was a manifestation of him. I concluded it was too important to trash or give away like many other things he had abandoned. What to do?

We had been together seventeen years when he found a girlfriend on the Internet who possessed some kind of gravitational pull. Just six weeks later he approached me with some lingo about an opportunity for him to go meet Doreen. I didn't know how to respond, so I didn't. *I be cooking supper here. My mother is here. I'm going to ignore this baffling suggestion.* He was determined, though, and pressed on as if encased in a confessional booth.

"I want to see her, but I am afraid I might do something stupid." I was stunned. *Seriously? That is messed up.*

I said, "You've already been stupid."

He glared at me, wobbling his head and looking incredibly arrogant and unapologetic. In spite of this attitude, I sensed his desperation. He had to go, but he wanted my permission. Finally, he said, "I really want to do this."

I really want you not to. "You need to know that if you go see D-o-r-e-e-n, you cannot come home to me." No doubt, he was going. He was already gone—like a freight train.

This discussion occurred in front of my eighty-one year old mother who was visiting. Why he decided to have this conversation in her presence was a mystery to me, but then the guy was not known for his sensitivity. She was sitting at the bar as I cooked supper when he sauntered up, sat down, and made the statement that he wanted to go meet Doreen. Mom asked, "Who is Doreen?" I ignored her because I didn't know how to answer that. When he said he was afraid he would do something stupid, Mom asked again,

"Who is Doreen?" And again, I ignored her question. As he pressed the issue, she persisted, "Who is this Doreen?" This time I answered. I looked at her squarely and issued a sharp, "Doreen is his girlfriend."

Mom had a way of huffing and puffing when something upset her. Clearly she was upset as her cheeks went in and out like a blowfish. To an Iowa farm woman, the scenario playing out in front of her was beyond her scope of comprehension. Clearly astonished and deeply troubled, she seemed to shrink in size as this information stormed into her. I felt sorrier for her than I did for me. I had no doubt, though, that her mother bear spirit was in there posturing to surface. She would not take the betrayal she witnessed lightly. As she always did, she would regroup and transform her vulnerable, fragile self into a rock.

Let me give some background on the relationship with my boyfriend. We both had become discontented with our lives, but neither of us did anything about it. It is true that when there is an interloper, the relationship is often already troubled. Ours was. During the many years we were together, his career regressed as mine took off. This introduced him to situations that were uncomfortable. He felt bad about it. I felt bad for him but was disappointed he couldn't fit in and support me. In addition, my accomplishments gave him no latitude to be my hero, which left him ripe for the plucking by a woman in crisis.

I can't speak to what other issues he might have had. There were undoubtedly legitimate ones. Since our breakup was swift and clean, I have no idea what swirled in his head other than Doreen. From my perspective, ours was a relationship that had run its course. He sent some strong signals that he felt the same way. Against my wishes he had started smoking cigars a couple of years earlier. (This was one of my non-negotiables, and he knew it). I begged him to stop. He wouldn't. I viewed this as a piercing affront. He became grumpy and withdrawn. He grew long hair and a beard, another affront. The gloominess in our home was pervasive, and I became cold and distant. Over time, our compatibilities vanished. I was go, go, go and he was cautious and slow—apathetic even. In spite of all this, I thought love was there. Apparently not.

He told me about his Internet friend the first day he connected with her. I didn't know what to make of that, so I just said, "Really?" After that, I got a spirited Doreen report every day when he got home from work. The relationship escalated quickly. He showed me pictures of her, and she had pictures of us. I felt somewhat violated. How did I become a part of this? I knew the evolving situation was weird, especially his out-of-character enthusiasm, but I was so mystified by it that I had no clue how to react. So I continued to say and do nothing. I believe that if I had tried to shut it down, he would have cheated. The fire was lit.

I knew instantly when the online relationship turned romantic. When they first connected on the Internet, he went from Mr. Grumpy to Mr. Cheerful overnight, but it was when he stopped the daily reports that I thought, *Wow, she landed him in a month.* Shortly thereafter, he got a hair cut, trimmed his facial hair, started working out, shopped at Abercrombie, switched out hot dogs and Cheetos for soup and fruit, and got a tan dark enough to be mistaken for a Middle Eastern terrorist.

When he began seeking treatment for his sleep disorder (something I had pleaded with him to do for years) and took up power walking (he wouldn't even walk with me), I was royally pissed. It irritated me that he did all the things for her he wouldn't do for me. Even though I knew the relationship had him all fired up, I didn't expect it to be so powerful he would give up what we had. I was wrong.

His laid-back nature made his betrayal especially shocking. This was a man I had to ask in February what his plan was to take down the outdoor Christmas lights. His new woman lit him on fire, which was annoying since I could not.

I decided early on I would not fight for him. His lust for someone else disgusted me, and I knew that no matter how things turned out with his new woman, I didn't want him anymore. A few days after he asked permission to see Doreen, I discovered him on the patio talking to her on the phone, so I ended it. *You cannot plant your fat ass on my patio and talk to your girlfriend.*

People hooking up on the Internet is not unusual today, but it was odd back then. The scenario unfolding was a mystery to me. Later that evening I asked him, "Who is this woman?" When he hissed, "Now I don't want you causing trouble for her," I bristled. *Did it not occur to you that she was causing trouble for me?* His concern only for her left no doubt. His loyalty had shifted. She owned him. I said, "Get out. Now."

I had no interest in having anything to do with her. He had a relationship with her. I did not. I was strangely uninterested in knowing anything about her, and there was no "sisterhood" consideration on her end for sure. There would be no tug-of-war over this man, and I was relieved that the glorious reports of their conversations had ended.

Throughout this ordeal, he was so distracted by his new love that he showed no signs of empathy for me. He only worried I would cause trouble and jeopardize his new deal. I was expendable. It was as though he woke up one day to find himself handcuffed to a dead hooker. With each suggestion of his shift in loyalty, another piece of my heart died until love was snuffed out. I lost my love, my home, and my life while he went coolly on his way, intoxicated with lust and passion. He was over the moon while I became entangled in a first wives' club mentality. And a plan took shape in my head.

While he boarded a plane for his romantic rendezvous, a moving van pulled up in front of our house. Friends and family converged. A realtor staked a "For Sale" sign in the yard. The house was priced to sell, and the realtor had buyers. I cared not about money. I just wanted it sold before he got back, possibly with his girlfriend in tow.

After my "get out" ultimatum, he immediately moved his personal things into an apartment in anticipation of his new love joining him there. Preoccupied with her, he had no interest in the things one accumulates when they have a big honking house and yard. My attorney girlfriends advised me that would change if he brought his girlfriend home with him. "They will start wanting stuff," they forewarned. *She may get my man, but she was **not** going to get my stuff.*

Anything I couldn't get in my new apartment was given to neighbors and friends. It wasn't a garage sale. It was a free sale. A purge. As they loaded things up, they said, "Let me know if you want this back later." I knew I never would. I needed it gone, as though the sacrifice of precious possessions would rid me of the gripping pain that festered inside. Soon there was a festive atmosphere about the whole process and everyone's energy blossomed. I was almost euphoric. The purge was cleansing. A sense of release swept over me. By the end of the day I had emptied out the house except for his red toolbox, which I left in the middle of the floor of the garage. It looked lonely sitting there as I closed the door for the last time.

Throughout the demise of this relationship, I tried to maintain my dignity and gracefully let go of that which was no longer mine, but I had cried incessantly as the episode unfolded. With a disturbing lack of empathy, my man interpreted my emotions as: "You are crazy." He only said that once, but it struck me like a sledgehammer. As the moving van pulled away from the beautiful home we designed and built together, I thought, *You ain't seen crazy yet*. Damaged and drained, I turned and looked back at my beautiful dream home and realized my dream had turned ugly and cruel. I didn't cry, though. I was through crying.

Later that night, wrapped in a soft comforter, I cried my heart out while curled in the fetal position on a plush rug in my luxurious loft apartment. The Tulsa skyline sparkled like mosaic crystals through panoramic windows framed with wispy sheer panels. City noise suggested an energy I would come to appreciate later, but not yet. The wounds were raw. Raging grief eventually settled into soft, muffled sobs that seemed to have no end. That night I learned that you don't stop crying when you decide you are not going to cry anymore. You stop crying when you stop crying.

When he returned from his rendezvous, he found the house empty and a sold sign in the front yard. He called me at work and asked where our stuff was. I told him I gave it away. He said, "You can't do that." I said, "So sue me."

A month later I was through crying. Instead, I broke out in some kind of crazy. I was better off without him, so why did I hurt so much over a man I was glad to have out of my life? Ego, I guess. I should have walked away sooner. Regretting my loyalty and commitment, I played the "if only" game in my head. Tortured, I called him and made a respectable fuss by insisting he tell me he was sorry.

Not for a moment did I want him back, but I craved an apology for the betrayal. He refused. He wasn't sorry. His new love was meant to be (as ours once was). I was wacko enough to scare him or shame him, I'm not sure which, and he finally said he was sorry. Sentimentality overcame me, and I told him I loved him, I had always loved him, and I loved him still, thereby proving that I was, in fact, crazy. Looking back I know he lied when he said he was sorry, and I lied when I said I loved him. I never cried over him again. A sense of peace settled in—the kiss of acceptance. A few days later I sent him a bottle of Fat Bastard wine.

In spite of this closure, a thickness of resentment continued to ripple though me. I rolled around in it for some time while wishing I were more noble. I was not noble. I sank into bitterness. Desperately clinging to my moral compass, I wondered if I could emerge with my dignity intact.

I don't regret the relationship. It was beautiful in the beginning, and a lot of good things came out of it. I just wish it had ended differently. The damage was deep. It took a full-court press to start life afresh. One of the things I did was buy a manly toolbox, a comprehensive set of tools, and a drill which I sometimes charge in my kitchen.

This breakup inched me toward The Crash. Dealing with men for forty years in a business environment not conducive to women also piled on layers of crusty man issues. The boys at work, with their testosterone-fueled engines, had the power and they used it. Fighting was sport. I fought the good fight, but I fought like a girl, and I got beat up. I prevailed in the end, though, at least partially.

chapter 6

FIGHT LIKE A GIRL

"Balls," said the Queen.
"If I had balls, I'd be king."

When I was promoted into management, an executive said, "A young buck should have that slot." It didn't matter that I had earned the promotion or that it was long overdue. My presence was a threat. I often wonder what my professional life would have been like if I were a man. No doubt my competence would have been assumed and a pack would have swept me along to prestigious exploits. For me, it wasn't like that. I had to prove myself and then some.

The "young buck" remark didn't represent the sentiments of all men. Generous congratulations were forthcoming, laced with, "You deserve it." But it did reflect the smoldering resentment of those threatened males who made my professional life a tortured triumph.

During a career spanning forty years, struggles were prolonged and exasperating. They left scars that complicated relations with men in the romance arena. It was one thing to endure men in suits in my professional life, and quite another to let them invade my personal one.

I rarely dated executives or businessmen. It was impossible to find my niche in such a relationship. As I got to know the wives of men I worked with, I understood why. They were, for the most part, wonderful women whom I admired, but I was not like them. I didn't know my place. I had no dependencies. I was in competition with men, and I was more like the men than like the women they loved. Operating in a harsh world, I had to put up barriers for protection that were impossible to penetrate on an emotional level. Buffeted and bruised, I grew hard.

When I retired, hard-won accomplishments and the pioneer woman persona of the work place contrasted starkly with my nebulous post-retirement identity. This exacerbated the sense of loss from the end of my career. Because I fought so hard for so long, this shift threw me off balance.

* * *

My career dreams materialized incrementally over many years. Although I ultimately rose from secretarial work to an executive position with a multi-billion-dollar company, I didn't have the foresight to set that as a goal when I started out. Women had been "in their place" forever, so I had no concept of the extent of possibilities. Only as I mastered one level did I see the prospect of the next one.

As a secretary/bookkeeper, my goal was to be an accountant, which was the ultimate accomplishment in my mind. When that was achieved, I set my sights on supervision, which I thought was the supreme achievement. That accomplished, I envisioned the possibility of manager and then director. Achieving those ranks, I believed that *they* would never let me be vice president, so I settled in.

This lack of ambition worked in my favor. (No white male wanted an ambitious minority in his upper level ranks.) I was non-threatening, so I got promoted to vice president. Again, I thought I had peaked but was later promoted to senior officer and placed on several boards.

My competency was obvious, except to the men who were not receptive to acknowledging it under any circumstances. Because of these non-believers, at one point my motivation for pursuing advancement shifted. Getting ahead ceased to be the primary driver. Beating the bullies was. I was getting beat up and, hugely pissed, I wasn't going to take it anymore. I began to fight. Mostly, I fought like a girl, proving myself with hard-earned results and avoiding conflict. But under attack I might aim for the balls.

In a situation where I was bullied by a peer, I stomped into his office, leaned over his desk, put a finger in his face (they hate that), and ranted. "No matter what you do, you are not running me off. I am not leaving. I am never, ever leaving. Rest assured, I'll be here when you are gone."

Allowing for no response, I marched out leaving him shocked and worried. What he had done was against company policy, and my atypical response cowered him. As I headed back to my office, he followed. "We can work something out," he pleaded.

"Fuck you very much," I responded.

In a meeting the next day he avoided my intimidating gaze. I gave him a break by not reporting him. I believe he appreciated that. Over time we became team players. My prediction was accurate. I was still there when he was gone.

* * *

Such challenges were not new to me. Men had marginalized my aspirations as far back as I can remember. Graduating from high school in 1962, I got a wild hair and told my father I wanted to go to college. He said, "You go to Des Moines and get a job at an insurance company until you get married like all the other girls. I've got boys to educate."

I didn't resent his response then, nor do I now. And I don't regret my acceptance of it. He reacted as the world had taught him, and I was strangled by female stereotypes. I'm not certain what a degree would have gotten me back then anyway. There were not a lot of career options for women. As a compromise of sorts, I worked my way through a secretarial program at a business school. I interpreted being a secretary as the pinnacle of success.

A young mother in my twenties in 1968, I worked as a secretary/bookkeeper at a high school. A senior girl helping in the office announced she was going to college to be an engineer. I was shocked. *Women can't be engineers. Or could they?* Her comment sparked an idea, and I began thinking about becoming an accountant.

Against my husband's wishes, I took night classes at a local college. My undergraduate degree was in business education because teaching was a profession he deemed acceptable. However, with a year of college left, we divorced, and I was no longer restricted by someone else's choice of my occupation. I began focusing on accounting.

To realize a career, many women paid the price of a failed marriage. I was one of them. The scope of this reality became clear years later when I put together a discussion panel for a women's conference. During Q&A, it was revealed that all but one of the executive women panelists were divorced, and they attributed the demise of their marriages to their professional ambitions. The message this conveyed to young women in the audience was disturbing, but it was reality.

* * *

When I first entered the workforce in the 1960s after graduating from business school, women functioned as servants to the potentates of business. Many labored in the office ghettos of steno and data entry pools. Others, like myself, acquiesced to the yoke of womanhood by being secretaries—babysitters to men in suits.

In 1975, I became degreed and entered corporate America where a backlash was lurking. Fueled by discontent, women found their voice and insisted on a law that required organizations to abandon policies which prohibited women from having certain jobs. This forced men into changes for which they were not prepared. Most didn't like it. Blatant prejudices became subversive, festering below the surface —hissing like radiators behind company public images.

As the women's movement ramped up, it spoke to me. I didn't march in the streets, but I did discreetly tap into the movement's critical mass and maniacal fury. My career was an uphill battle from there on out, but I was up for it. Even the tough times had a certain appeal. I saw myself as a pioneer woman, and I embraced the struggle.

Divorced and on my own, I landed a job in Tulsa as a petroleum accountant at an oil company. Executives there were seeking a mature women to invade a bullpen of male accountants staunchly entrenched in the world they created. The old guys had run off several young girls fresh out of college. (You don't have to blow much cigar smoke in the face of a twenty-two-year-old young lady to get her to leave.) I was thirty-one and more likely to survive the smoke-filled, testosterone-rich bullpen.

Hoping I would stick, *they* threw me in with a bunch of cigar and pipe smoking old geezers. Sizing up the situation, I concluded it didn't look hopeful, but desperate for a job to support my family, I was determined to make it work. I had a couple of advantages in that regard. First, I was fresh out of a difficult divorce with two children to raise. Emotionally on edge, I was pathetic. I showed up at work with eyes swollen, making excuses about allergies. The old codgers saw through that and felt sorry for me.

Second, I had an affinity for old men. When I was a child, Mom occasionally sent me to retrieve Dad from the town tavern. His buddies fussed over me, and my fascination with old men began. So at work, when Chester leaned down, took aim, threw his eraser under my desk, and eased himself out of his office chair to retrieve it, I was not offended, but I did tell him to "Get the hell out of here."

I followed up by throwing the eraser, hitting Chester in the back if my aim was good. If not, Wilbur might take a hit. This scene was entertaining to bullpen characters and was repeated numerous times.

When Frank blew cigar smoke in my face, I took a bite out of the apple on his desk. He always got the better of me, though. I offered to share a box of Valentine candy. I had taken a bite out of every piece. He studied the assortment briefly and then licked every one.

In another incident, I caught him staring at my breasts. I made a smart remark about them not being real and that I had bought them at a hardware store. He told me I should have gotten them both in the same size. Touché. That was 1976. Sexual harassment legislation was passed in 1974, but it took years for courts to define it. That episode would have gotten both of us in trouble today.

The desks were crunched together in sets of two facing each other in a long, narrow room. Marvin's desk faced mine. Leaning back in his chair while on the phone one day, he noticed a string on his fly. He picked up a huge pair of scissors designed to cut green-bar computer paper and positioned it in his crotch area with one hand while holding the phone in the other. Marvin working those monster scissors around his fly to catch and cut the string was a bizarre sight. I pleaded, "No, Marvin, don't do it. Please don't do it." The guys loved it.

When I began dating, the old fellows lived vicariously through my misadventures as a divorcée. A single woman in their midst was almost more than they could stand. They badgered me on Mondays for stories about weekend escapades. I made up tales to entertain, and they checked the obituaries to determine if any of the men for whom I cooked dinner died. They became my allies, my distraction, and my friends. The office became a healing place where I could get away from personal struggles. And I became the woman who stayed.

Passed over for promotions, I was told the men candidates were more qualified. They weren't. So I set out to obtain so many credentials that I could not be turned down when opportunities to move up were available. This involved getting an M.B.A., becoming a C.P.A., attending Toastmasters meetings at six in the morning, and working overtime as needed. I did all this while raising children alone. It was draining. I needed another day between Saturday and Sunday. Looking back, I wonder how I did it.

It took six years of night classes to get an M.B.A. Studying for the C.P.A. exam was an intense three-year effort, and I had to take thirty hours of accounting courses to qualify to take the test. During this time, I went to work early, and by the time everyone else arrived, I had studied for three hours. My children independently got themselves to school. After work, I went to night classes. Weekends were spent studying, doing research, and writing papers. Exhausted, at times when the alarm went off in the mornings, I cried.

After passing the C.P.A. exam, I couldn't stand to look at the study materials anymore, so I threw them into a closet. That wasn't enough, so I covered them with a blanket. I was spent. I called Mom to tell her I passed the test. This Iowa farm woman—who at my age was canning peaches, feeding hogs, and butchering chickens while raising five kids—said, "That's nice. What is a C.P.A.?" Dad's comment was, "You should have been a boy." The fact that I had no one with whom to share success became painfully clear. I celebrated by buying my kids new bicycles.

My lofty aspiration at that time was to be a supervisor, but it wasn't happening. So I took a job at another firm. The director of the division tried to convince me to stay. "We have our eyes on you for supervisor here," he said.

"When might that happen?"

"In about five years."

Amazed, I asked, "Why would I wait that long when I can have that down the street now?" He had no answer for that, and I was off.

* * *

My career was positively influenced by the desolate state of my love life. Disenchanted with the dating scene, I became convinced no white knight was going to rescue me. If I wanted something, I had to get it myself. I wanted a professional career and a good life for my children. So I developed a plan to achieve those goals and executed it. Fiercely independent, I didn't need anybody—not a good formula for love but a good one for a career.

My single status was a double-edged sword. It freed me to go after goals without inhibitions from a spouse, but it made me different from peers whose wives took care of the details of life, supported their efforts, and managed their children. I was on my own. I never envied them, though. I valued my independence.

I bounced around from job to job throughout my thirties. Each move was a step up. Much in demand as a troubleshooter, I could fix a broken accounting system. I had a knack for turning a mess into a "lean, mean, running machine," and each time I did it, I got better at it. When I hit my forties, I moved from accounting to operations and settled into a challenging corporate environment in a complex industry. It was there that I began a serious climb into the executive ranks. I found my niche, and the pioneering kicked in big time.

I took over an ailing department and fixed it, and then another, and another. At the peak, I managed hundreds of people, served on boards, and ran operations for subsidiaries—a perfect match of aptitude to company needs. It was then that I discovered how it feels to do what you were born to do.

As I moved into the highest ranks of the organization, detractors tried to slap a token woman label on me, but it didn't stick. No one gave me anything. I earned everything I got, and then some. Every break I got should have come sooner than it did. Still, when important assignments were given to me, someone invariably questioned whether a woman could do the job. Through the grapevine I heard the complaints and predictions of failure. "They will eat her alive," one said after I was given a challenging customer to deal with.

That didn't happen. I built strong business relationships and took on projects no one else would touch. My bosses, for the most part, became my champions. One said, "Give her something to do, grab a hold of the back of her hair, and hold on." In spite of the innuendo, I took that as a compliment. Although some men were supportive, it was never to the degree of being a mentor. Such a relationship would have created problems for them, and I never sought that deep a connection.

Concerns about women's capabilities were not limited to men. Women were conditioned to view men as overseers and were apprehensive about a woman boss. Their attitudes changed over time as I found talented women in the ranks and began mentoring, coaching, and promoting them— something men didn't do.

* * *

My overall strategy for success was to walk a fine line between being effective and non-threatening. I cultivated strong production and project teams but moderated any cheerleading about their accomplishments. Men could walk around with graphs and reports and bluster about successes, but that didn't work well for me.

While men's credibility was usually assumed, it took years for me to be viewed as credible. On one occasion, my boss told me outright he didn't believe a report I submitted on the success of a project. He wasn't buying the data, although it was independently verified. I learned to let results speak for themselves over time. I knew what my team had accomplished, and I developed my own recognition processes.

A key component to fighting like a girl was to not buy into male beliefs that made no sense. One of them was men's interpretation of weakness. "Never let them see you bleed," one advised. Any display of fear or worry was not in their repertoire. Crying ended careers. I never considered a career over because someone cried at work, man or woman.

Most men interpreted changing your mind as a weakness, so they stubbornly held their positions no matter what. They never saw the foolishness in this. I had no problem changing my mind when information suggested it, and I never held it against anyone else when they did so.

Most men saw collaboration as a weakness as well. They preferred "I got you" sport over teaming up. The perception of men as team players is overrated. They compete vigorously with teammates, sometimes overlooking the common goal. (Plenty of politicians prove this point.)

Some men were territorial and responded defensively when problems were identified in their areas. These men were so consistent in their reactions that their behavior was amazingly predictable. They threw up decoys to distract from problems and attacked messengers. I taught other employees how to interact with them, "Sit in his office, anchor yourself in a chair, and take the verbal beating. Don't leave. Eventually you'll get what you need. You just have to go through the bullshit grinder to get it."

Such men might discreetly fix a problem, but they would never admit it existed. Or they would blame it on someone else. In contrast, I welcomed input from any source on problems, took accountability for failures and mistakes, and got all over fixing them. It's tough to fix a problem if you don't acknowledge it.

Most men believed you always back your employees no matter what. This rewarded bad behavior, promoted a lack of accountability, stymied personal growth, and created assholes. I never defended bad behavior. Instead, I helped employees develop the courage to face up to their mistakes, fix them, and grow from them. That was progress.

Many men were bullshit aficionados who believed "I don't know" was a sign of weakness. Steadfastly confident, they would fake it till they made it. These men interpreted my "I don't know, but I'll find out" approach as weakness.

When I disagreed with a proposal to come before a committee, I approached the man proposing it beforehand rather than introducing an "I got you" dynamic into a meeting. This allowed him to re-think his position, tweak it, or develop counter arguments to mine. This approach promoted good decisions and sped up the decision-making process, but it was interpreted by some as weakness.

* * *

In spite of these irritants, men were generally jokesters and fun to work with. Their alpha male contact sports backgrounds taught them that everything is a game, so they didn't take things personally. That is, unless they decided to take something personally, in which case, look out.

For me, vulnerability worked better than trying to present a strong front. Although I was careful not to go into the victim mode (you give away your power when you do that), I was not afraid to engage in self-deprecating humor.

The company president took a team to lunch at an upscale restaurant. Afterward, we lingered in the parking garage while valets retrieved cars. A black Lincoln was delivered. I got in it and drove off. At a stoplight a man began banging on the car window. Although certain he wanted me, I ignored him. He was a nice looking fellow but a bit too animated for my taste. Then I realized what he was yelling. "You're in my car!" Noting unfamiliar items in the console, I relinquished the vehicle.

While feeling the sting of the reality that he didn't want me, I tried to maintain my dignity as I walked confidently back into the garage, high heels clicking authoritatively on the concrete. There the team was bent over with laughter. Shortly after, a valet brought up a sleek red sports car. An old man limped out to it. The president said "Run, Nikki. You can beat him." This story was resurrected every year at the annual luncheon, and I laughed as heartily as anyone.

More important than any non-threatening tactics, though, was competency. I read somewhere that if a person invested thirty minutes a day studying a topic, they would be an expert in a year. So I spent many lunch hours poring over industry reading materials. I soon became an expert, even on a national level, and I shared everything I learned with my team and others.

Employee development was a top priority. Any investment in people yielded significant returns, and I often did training hands on. This required many extra hours of work. My rationale for spending time this way was that the synergy generated from highly trained employees might make training the most important thing I did all week. I also studied how to match employees' aptitudes to the work at hand. This produced an optimal workforce, stronger teams, efficiency gains, and loyal, energized employees. These capabilities were the source of my influence, and they set me apart.

* * *

It was generally not productive to complain about discrimination or mistreatment. Doing so just made me look bad while accomplishing nothing. This was because many of the incidents were minor. Standing alone, they may have been inconsequential, but in unrelenting waves, a woman could drown in them. This produced a no-win situation. If I complained about a single event, I appeared petty. If I reported a stream of incidents, I was whining, making something out of nothing, and laying it on.

A man responsible for facility support at one company played this to his advantage brilliantly. Minor abuses from him and his staff were constant and cumulative. They were effective at disrupting my departments. My office fell into such ill repair that my secretary named it *The Rain Forest*. I scheduled meetings and interviews in conference rooms because no one worth hiring would accept a job offer if they saw the condition of my office. This went on for years. Finally, one day the president made a rare appearance in my office. "Come with me," he said.

He led me to the executive floor and pointed to my name on a plaque on the door of my new office. I was thrilled, but I had no doubt that if I were a man, I would have already been there. My peers were there. I wondered what happened to draw his attention to my predicament. I never got the answer to that question, but the abuse stopped.

Double standards existed all over the place. At one company, men of my rank had company cars. I was told I didn't drive enough business miles to qualify for one, but men had them who drove fewer miles than I did. When I pressed the issue, it was suggested that the problem be solved by taking everyone's car away. Well played. This would have made me immensely unpopular with peers. You have to give it to the guys. That was a brilliant tactic. It shut me up.

I received a couple of extremely large raises over the years because my salary was out of line with peers. Each time I wondered how long I had been underpaid. Men sent kids to universities with college funds while I cash flowed mine. As a retiree now, I wonder how much better my counterparts are living because of being paid more all those years. These salary disparities were finally remedied only because of lawyers who pointed out penalties for ignoring equal pay legislation. Without those interventions, men in power would have no doubt been content with my diminished worth without giving it a second thought.

Companies eventually embraced zero tolerance for sexual harassment. In the early days, though, dirty stories were rampant. As things changed, the boys found it difficult to give up the off-color jokes. During a long ride with men in a carpool, I endured an episode of verbal assaults via raunchy stories. At one point it occurred to one of them to ask if I was offended. I said, "Not as long as none of you, *never ever* make me mad." That cooled their jets, and a robust conversation about BB guns broke out.

Any woman who took the legal route had to be prepared to give up everything. I believe I was once promoted because another woman filed a discrimination suit. Tulsa is a small town, and such an action could end a career. One gutsy woman made that brave sacrifice. With an impending investigation facing the company, executives looked for a woman to promote. I was that woman. That promotion was overdue, and I was primed and ready.

I held my ground when circumstances dictated but picked fights carefully. Some were not going to be won, and in those cases, I admit to ignoring maltreatment and exploitation. Instead, I chose to be a subtle provoking influence—treading delicately through the minefield. The appropriateness of this could be argued, but my entry into the highest ranks of a corporation supports that strategy.

Although somewhat timid in the early years, as I gained credibility I called men out when they expressed biased perceptions. A male co-worker was livid because a woman got a job for which he had applied. He went into a tirade at lunch. (It was common for men to assume that when a woman got promoted it was because she was a token and less qualified than male candidates. In truth, few women were tokens. They generally had to prove themselves longer, be more qualified, and out-perform the men in order to be promoted.) He said, "She got that job because she's a woman, and that's not fair."

I said to my friend, "I *did not* get jobs because I *was* a woman, and I'm certain she *didn't* as well. That's not fair either. Furthermore, men get jobs because they *are* men, and you are complaining to the wrong person."

On another occasion, a man complained that he had a horrible woman boss. I asked him, "When you have a horrible man boss, do you refer to him as a horrible *man* boss or just a horrible boss?"

I protested to a company owner who would not allow women employees to have maternity benefits even though a law required it. Company policy provided these benefits only for the wives of the men who worked there. He said, "No one asked those women to get pregnant." I quit over that issue, although the problems were deeper than that. I was never going to move up in that company. Management positions were filled with frat boys fresh out of college or good-old-boy buddies.

I was topped out at managing a group of women accountants, whom the men considered clerks because they were women. No doubt they considered me one as well. So I left to work for a company I thought provided better opportunities. It didn't. Discrimination was pervasive. There was no getting away from it.

I eventually left that company as well when the owners said I could not be promoted because the financial people they did business with in New York wouldn't relate to a woman. This was an excuse for their own biases. In fact, the New Yorkers were shocked at the way women were treated in both Oklahoma and Texas. They told me so.

I was called into a meeting (from which I was excluded—I was a girl) to answer financial questions. I wore a silk blouse and hadn't taken time to put on my jacket. As I stood there explaining financial reports, the company owner, a randy fellow, interrupted me to point out that one of my nipples was hard and the other was not. Of course, this stopped me dead in my tracks, and an awkward hush filled the room. The other men were as shocked as I was.

I solved the problem by tweaking the lazy nipple, setting it free of whatever constraint caused the problem, and resumed my financial report. I imagined the New Yorkers telling that story back home and cringed at the image it painted of Oklahoma. If I had not been so complicit in my response, I could have possibly won a lawsuit over the incident, especially with all those New York witnesses. Had I done so, though, I would have never worked in this town again. Not long after, I left that company. I never experienced that level of uncouth behavior again, but other challenges continued unimpeded.

A company hired me to fix their "fucked up" accounting system (their quote, not mine), and I did. I cleaned it up, ran the accounting department for two years, and filled in for an absent comptroller for almost a year. In spite of that, the comptroller position was eventually filled with a less qualified man who spent his time on long lunches and golf. When his work began to flow back into my office, I complained and was told, "He doesn't know how to do it." When the comptroller position had been vacant and I took over, I hadn't known how to do it either, but I learned.

I remembered a Yogi Berra quote my Dad used, "If you come to a fork in the road, take it." I never understood what that quote meant until that day. I quit—walked out.

The economy was bad at the time and my boss told me I'd never find another job in that market. I said, "I'd rather make tacos than work here another day." It was a good job that paid well, so quitting was one of the riskiest things I ever did, but it was also one of the grandest. As I walked across the parking lot to my car, I jumped up and clicked my heels together like the guy in the movie *Midnight Express* when he got out of a Turkish jail. Unbelievably, within a year the company tried to hire me back. Their accounting system was "fucked up" again.

That was the last time I quit a job. My taking my marbles and going home when unappreciated was abandoned. Changing companies just traded one problem for another, so I introduced staying power into my portfolio of strategies and developed coping tactics. Endurance became my credo.

* * *

The arduous structure of the corporate environment was confining, and my identity was wrapped up in it for thirty-some years. In 2007 at sixty-two, I was ready to escape, and I announced my retirement.

Toward the end of my career, I got in trouble at work for swearing. I answered a question too candidly when a group of women asked me about getting ahead through relationships with men. I warned, "Know this. You cannot fuck your way to the top." I could have made that point more delicately, but the conversation occurred after work hours, and I assumed informality. However, a woman in the group was offended and filed a complaint. I felt betrayed and pulled back on mentoring women after that. In an interview for the company newsletter, I was asked what I was going to do to celebrate my retirement. I said, "I'm going to smoke pot and swear." Needless to say, my response did not appear in the publication.

When I left the workforce, the fight ended. The absence of stress from grinding challenges was breathtaking, and a sense of relief settled over me. When the morning news revealed bad weather or frustrating traffic, I sipped coffee, looked out the window, and gloated.

I didn't miss the world I lived in for so long—the world I helped create. I did my pioneer woman thing, I did it well, and I was relieved to not have to do it anymore. I was no longer that person: the queen of productivity and efficiency, the results-oriented fiend, the leader going for the win. I didn't know it then, but I was on my way to becoming somewhat of an old hippie who focuses on inconsequential things such as how to avoid being degraded and abused (not necessarily in that order) by a crossword puzzle.

This signaled a problem, though. Fighting like a girl was a passion. After retirement, I had no passion. I missed the intensity. I missed being part of a team. I missed claiming victory over intimidating challenges. In spite of the tribulations of those career years, they were halcyon days. The thrill of accomplishment, the rewards of raising children, and the fun of being single and independent were sweet. And it was gone. All gone.

chapter 7

WRT (WOMAN RIGHT THERE)

Men in packs.

As I moved into the executive ranks, my presence created waves. When I attended an executive meeting for the first time, the men began planning their annual fishing trip. Suddenly, the president looked at me as though he saw me for the first time. There was a WRT (Woman Right There). This produced an awkward moment. The revelation ping-ponged around the room until every man got it. You would have thought a corpse had sat up in a coffin.

I quickly interjected, "I have no interest in fishing, and I don't want to ruin your fun. Go ahead. Go fishing." They didn't, and that was the end of the fishing trips, at least as far as I knew. The guys were good at sneaking around. They labeled afterwork socials as charity planning events, more to fool their wives than to exclude women at the office. Some played their wives like fine guitars. When I worked on weekends at one company, men were frequently in the office watching sports on television. This puzzled me until they explained that they faked work so their wives and kids would feel sorry for them and do the yard work.

I had no interest in another manly pastime—golf. This was a significant handicap because important bonds were formed on golf courses. I was told I would have to take it up if I wanted to get ahead, but I simply could not bring myself to do it. I was also told I should get married. I refused to comply with either suggestion and had a successful career anyway. I went on business golf trips with the fellows and occupied myself with reading, shopping, and sitting around a pool. As for getting married, well, I just couldn't do it, at least not for that reason.

I was at a golf resort with men from work when one of them asked me to pick up Titleist golf balls for him at the pro shop. Not a golfer, I realized as I entered the shop that I couldn't remember the brand name of the golf balls. I was relieved to run into men from the office who were enthusiastic about helping me out with the name. They advised, "It's Trojans. They are the best."

I knew from the look on the clerk's face when I asked for Trojan balls that I'd been had. The men from the office snickered in the corner behind a rack of pink and yellow golf pants. The incident was a topic of conversation at dinner that night.

I gave as good as I got. I gave one of those men a ride to lunch one day. It was over 100 degrees. I turned on the passenger seat warmer and took the long route. He sweated like a man in a Russian sauna.

* * *

There was little strain on work relationships with men in the early days of my career when, as a secretary, I was an *office wife* babysitting men. I knew my place. Although I did have to take a stand against swats on the butt and a few other demeaning behaviors from spirited men, these incidents were handled without animosity. It was when I transitioned from secretarial work to a professional career that my presence rankled some men, and they were not afraid to express how they felt.

Antagonists peddled distorted tales that tainted the perceptions of reasonable men who were on the fence about my presence. At times I wanted to thump the fear mongers on their heads or worse. I didn't because I had no desire to work in a prison library. Instead, I fantasized about painting their toenails while they slept.

The guys most receptive to my presence found it awkward to reveal their support, so they usually didn't. Men travel in packs, and maintaining a position in the pack was vital to their own achievement. So while I advanced into management, powerful pack influences dampened visible and enthusiastic endorsements of anything I did.

I *got* the pack mentality. My whole life involved grappling with them. Raised as the only girl in a brood of brothers, I learned at an early age that survival of pack members depended on their standing together against a perceived threat. This was vividly revealed when my little brother, whom I practically raised, aligned himself for the first time with my other brothers who were excluding me. It hurt, but what was he to do when they pulled the ladder up into the treehouse? He was a boy.

I grew up observing the dynamics of male pack leaders and their followers in church, school, and in families. My marriage reflected those established roles. When divorced, I continued to find myself attracted to men tightly bonded in packs. There was something appealing about the power of the pack and the persona it evoked. I acquiesced to it in my personal life, but in the professional arena, pack behavior was so damaging that it was beyond annoying. I understood it, though, possibly better than the pack members themselves. This awareness was a valuable leveler.

I launched my professional career in corporate America in the 1970's, and faced the quintessential pack—the good-old-boy network. A contentious relationship was inevitable. However, I appreciated the men's perspective. With a female in their territory, the pack closed ranks against a threat, and occasionally they attacked.

When the pack went into attack mode, even the best of men participated in harassment or ignored it. Like my little brother, no one was going to take my side. I was sympathetic to the dilemma of those who supported me but would not speak out. Their empathetic glances in meetings when the pack was being the pack and I was going to pay were noted and appreciated.

On occasion a man took a stand. The chairman of a meeting insisted on no restroom breaks. Men could go all morning or afternoon without a break. I could not. So I left the meeting briefly. When I returned, I expected a disgruntled chairman. Instead it was dead dog quiet. Later I learned one of the men took up for me. From then on out, when I had to go, I went, and so did everyone else. What a relief.

Most of the time, I let the guys have their *man issues.* I didn't take them on. Instead, I focused on taking care of employees and customers and delivering solid outcomes. It was futile to try to fit in, so I didn't try. I had no interest in invading the good-old-boy network. There were benefits to not being distracted by the politics of the pack and to not being subjected to typical male behaviors.

The differences between the style of men and women in the work environment are numerous and beyond the scope of this book. In general, though, men aspire to be powerful while women seek influence. I first realized this when the president of a company projected his motives onto me and accused me of seeking power when I asked for more staff. Power was the furthest thing from my mind. In fact, it hadn't even occurred to me. I wanted to take care of customers and take some pressure off employees. He could not comprehend that motive.

I took a more collaborative approach to projects than most men and sidestepped the competitive "I got you" sport they enjoyed. When possible, I avoided competition and confrontation, and I overlooked a lot. When I did fight, I fought like a girl. That meant delivering results.

I focused on long-term solutions and developed human resources, which distinguished me from men. They mainly chased an immediate big splash that would impress and get them promoted. They seemed unaware of the messes they left behind and showed little interest in employee issues. Their focus was on symptoms rather than root causes. Incentives were mostly based on easily achieved short-term goals. If they could score a few wins, they could move up. The good-old-boy network would carry them along. Permanent solutions required taking risks, installing systems and processes, and developing staff. Those solutions take time and work, and sometimes you have to break something to fix it. I was not afraid to do that, and the sacrifices and processes required to redeem an operation were my forte.

Most men harbored a detached attitude toward the employees who were not in their upwardly mobile pack. This included the WRTs. They didn't see women as having potential. When I hired men, the guys noticed them and recruited them into their areas with promotions while capable women were ignored. Both the men and the women accepted this in the early years. I stirred the pot when I identified the crackerjack women and promoted them.

To adapt to the male dominated environment, many career-oriented women took on manly behaviors and avoided the championing of women. They aspired to be part of the good-old-boy networks. By not doing so, I eventually ingratiated myself to women employees. I further charmed them with speeches at employee events where I made fun of the annoying sports analogies men favored. I used housekeeping and childrearing ones, much to the delight of the mostly female workforce.

* * *

I was severely disadvantaged because of limited access to important players. As a woman, I couldn't walk into my boss's office with coffee and chat every day like the men did. Doing so would have created pack issues for the man in addition to rumors and innuendoes. Because of this disparity of access, hostile males told distorted tales about me, and I had no opportunity to counter them. This was damaging and isolating. Also, I avoided after work socializing because I was cognizant of wives worrying about their men socializing with women from the office. It is common today. Back then, it was not.

I sometimes have a twinge of regret that I didn't give the boys more trouble. Should I have pounded the table and thrown hissy fits? Should I have plunked my ass down in some guy's office with a coffee cup and not left until I'd covered all the gossip and issues of the day and to hell with the consequences? Should I have cultivated a mentor relationship and let the chips fall where they may? Should I have drunk beer and smoked cigars at happy hours? If I had done so, would the men have been less intimidated by the WRT? Probably not.

A man revealed his fear of the presence of women when one was promoted. He complained, "We're going to have a bunch of damn women running this company." (This was a prospect far removed from reality.) When a key management position opened up in my area, an all-woman entry-level department, he instructed me to hire a man "to balance out the team." This was in spite of a plethora of solid internal women candidates. I responded, "I'll balance my team when you balance the executive floor." The senior executive ranks were filled with all white men. His expression revealed his shock at my boldness. Eventually, this man became an enthusiastic champion of diversity and the closest thing to a mentor I ever had.

Over the years, pack behavior moderated, and some of the men who gave me the most grief in the beginning became my biggest champions. Women softened the edges of the business world and introduced rational shifts in thinking. How men reacted to this initially was driven by the culture that shaped them. Over time, men and women together transformed that culture. We changed the world for our daughters, granddaughters, and beyond. We were pioneers. I'm proud of those men and what we did.

* * *

I sought tactics to moderate my resentment toward men. One was to imagine them as small children romping on a playground or interacting in a classroom. In meetings I visualized pompous ass executives as posturing little roosters at school but vulnerable, bullied innocents at home. Analytical men were seen as quiet, serious little organizers and thinkers with bad haircuts and big ears trying to find their place in a world that didn't value their redeeming qualities. High energy, fun-loving guys were viewed as spirited negotiators working deals on the playground and hyped-up wigglers in the classroom.

I stared into the eyes of men around a boardroom table as they postured, made themselves big, and dished out intimidating gazes, and I imagined the eyes of children. I considered their faults and how they must have pained and challenged their parents. I was mindful that every man was some mother's son. These men were once little people shaped by the world in which they lived, one that considered women second class citizens.

When I retired, work relationships faded quickly, and I no longer had the distraction of a profession when other parts of my life took a nosedive. In severe contrast to the career years, the world began to view me as irrelevant. I accepted that presumption, just as I accepted my place as a young woman when I gave up my dream of college. When my retirement dreams of writing were stymied by technical issues, I found myself on a fast track to The Crash.

chapter 8

TECHNOLOGY SPANKED ME

I will go kicking and screaming into the digital age,
and I'll take whatever medication is required to do so,
or I will concede defeat and accept dinosaur status.

After retirement and giving up men, I got engaged to a computer, which was an experience similar to hazing. A counselor nurturing a five-year-old through his parents' divorce asked, "Tommy, are you feeling overwhelmed?" Tommy pondered the question briefly and then responded excitedly to the revelation it produced, "Yes. Yes. I have too many whelms." That's how I felt when confronted with a computer. I had too many whelms.

The help desk support I enjoyed at the office was gone and technology became like a suitcase without handles. Desperate to realize writing dreams and to connect with others through email and social media, I tried to embrace technology. When that didn't go well, dreams faded and an isolating disconnectedness set in. This ineptitude in the digital arena contributed to the loss of my moxie.

Technology, my window to the world, had the power to make me "suddenly old" in a keystroke. As I grappled with this modern-day tormentor, I frequently echoed words my mother used to describe herself in her final years, "You old fool." While I lamented my incompetence, I also felt sorry for the technically astute young people who exhibited unfortunate behaviors online. At least the stupid stuff I did in my youth occurred before the Internet existed.

Though barely out of the toddler stage, my grandchildren were more technically proficient than I. This was humbling. When at a restaurant with my family one day, my purse was stocked with small toys with which to distract my two-year-old granddaughter if she got restless. However, when signs of the jitters hit, her father slipped her his cell phone, which she took to like a duck on a June bug. The toys in my purse held little appeal. This diminutive little girl swiped her tiny fingers across the screen, selected apps, and played games with the concentration and dexterity of a trained technician. She had me beat, and she was only two.

Another granddaughter climbed up in a chair and pecked away at a computer keyboard. When her mother approached, the tyke pounded frantically to get in as many keystrokes as possible before Mom got there. This resulted in an attempted security breach of some sort. A flashing screen message said, "You do not have sufficient permission to do that." To be sure, she would soon be using technology with permission in ways I could not even imagine. To connect with grandchildren, somehow I had to come to terms with the digital world. The problem was that technology had me lassoed into a state of frustration and fear on the level of discovering a tarantula in the bathtub.

When I had a job, support staff assisted with technical issues. When Viagra and penile implant advertisements hit my email, I forwarded them to the company security officer with the comment, "You might be interested in this." (After retirement, I forwarded them to ex-boyfriends.) Without their support, and knowing technology was not my friend, I recognized the need to protect myself, so I found myself a technical genius, whom I called the Dalai Geek.

I asked, "What is a virus? What does it mean if I get one?"

He said, "A virus is someone fucking with you. When you get one, you are fucked."

Well, okay. That didn't sound good. It meant I could expect to get screwed over sooner or later by hardware and software. And that is pretty much what happened.

I was afraid of the Internet. People seemed to disappear into it and never come back. It alienated me from those who became technical enthusiasts. A friend on a social media site asked me to water corn on his virtual farm while he was on vacation. The way I saw it, anyone who farmed on a computer could water his own damn corn.

Futile fights with the computer left me victimized, battered, and afraid. That fear ruined my days and chipped away at my self-esteem. With a barrage of problems and immense frustrations, I dreaded every interaction with the computer and spent a fortune on geeks. When one problem was solved, another surfaced. "What's wrong?" I asked the Dalai Geek.

"You have too many tabs open on your browser."

"What is a browser?"

He explained that, and I asked, "What is a tab?"

He explained other dark mysteries of the digital world, which were impossible to understand, let alone remember.

Then he said, "That'll be $85."

"Thank you."

The Internet facilitated all manner of intrusions into my life. I felt continuously invaded and violated. Emails from tourists trapped in Nigeria with no money, broken backs, and kidney failures beseeched me. I checked my credit report online after which I began receiving forty-some solicitations daily for ski trips, student loans, and other non-viable financial opportunities for a woman my age—a nuisance on the level of mosquitoes.

An embarrassing phishing expedition debacle robbed me of my dignity and a week of my life. An Internet bandit hacked into my computer and sent an email that asked everyone in my contact list to send money—a scam. Then the worm tortured everyone in my contact file by doing the same thing to them. This made me look like an idiot and caused my friends to wish they didn't know me and their friends to wish they didn't know them, and their friends to wish . . . It was a fiasco. I lost several days of my life trying to recover. This traumatic personal violation and the threat of a repeat experience kept me in a perpetual state of feeling like a shelf sagging from too much weight. It also kept the Dalai Geek in business.

"That'll be $85."

"Thank you."

I was just as technically challenged when I worked, but I was not alone. I had an assistant and help desk support. Also, even in that environment no one could master the entire spectrum of technical components. Techies had to narrow their scope and specialize in certain aspects. In a meeting, the company president asked a technical guy a question. The man, who looked painfully uncomfortable and preferred to be in the bowels of the company having a relationship with hardware and software, didn't have the answer. He responded, "I'm just a mainframe kinda guy."

Later a PC network guy was asked a question he couldn't answer and declared, "I'm just a PC kinda guy."

When asked a question, I followed suit and replied, "I'm just a dumb terminal kinda gal." And I was.

The terminal was a big honkin' contraption on my desk that was stupid. The intelligence resided in a mainframe the size of a railroad car in a hermetically sealed room somewhere in the building. Both devices collaborated to ruin my life and career. This resulted in a constant flow of technical geniuses in my office in a perpetual state of rescuing me.

This technical support was not without problems. A young expert with a new vibrating pager was on his back under my computer desk fixing wiring. When his pager went off for the first time, the kid thought he was being electrocuted. He yelped and came scooting out, arms and legs flailing like a crab being chased by a dog on the beach. Sitting at my desk, I dodged this scrambling technician as he scooted toward me.

I had no idea what inspired his bizarre behavior, but I was not attracted to men with the capacity to create a virus, so I was taken aback by his sudden movement in my direction. I reacted by maneuvering my oversized leather executive chair with highly engineered rollers through a diversion process that would have made any fighter pilot proud.

My secretary responded to the commotion by rushing into the room to discover a technician wrapped around the base of my chair, his privates precariously close to the rollers. I was leaning back with my feet in the air in an awkwardly provocative position. When he sat up, the situation worsened, and I climbed over the arm rest onto the credenza like a critter being snapped at by an alligator.

* * *

At home, such traumas were avoided, but there were problems. The printer was a menace. Before I learned how to cancel printing, I experienced episodes of massive unanticipated output. As I stood helplessly by, page after page spit forth. It's not good to expect one page and get forty. These incidents caused the printer to run out of ink, which required another level of technical expertise I did not possess at the time.

"That'll be $85," said the Dalai Geek.

"Thank you."

Even when things worked like they were supposed to, technology was befuddling. I never understood why so many wires were bunched up behind a computer configuration that was wireless. It looked like a telephone company switching station back there. Also, my computer had a tendency to hibernate—a ridiculous concept for an electronic device. But hibernate it did—often.

The PC was courteous and warned me when it decided to do so. The first time it gave me the message *"preparing to hibernate,"* I couldn't believe it. *Really? Really? You are going to hibernate? That's rich.*

At this point I named my computer *It* (a name I once used for an old boyfriend who pretty much hibernated every weekend on my sofa). *It* locked up frequently, and when it did, I had to play solitaire manually with a deck of cards until the Dalai Geek showed up. Even he couldn't determine the source of the problem. At one point he blamed it on hardware, and then software, and then the computer overheating from being on a granite countertop. I found it difficult to accept that a monster with the mean-spirited temperament of my computer could have such a delicate constitution.

After each visit The Dalai Geek said, "That'll be $85."

"Thank you."

Every time I thought I was on a roll as a hot techie momma, something else happened, but I didn't know what happened. I would hit a key and "Whoa!" "Whoops." "Oh my!" "Surprise!"

"You are up and running," the Dalai Geek would say. "That'll be $85."

"Thank you."

Repeat, repeat, repeat. Hurt and defeated, I cried as I hunted for my snuggie, which the people who live in my attic had hidden along with my remote, reading glasses, car keys, and slippers. Technology won—again. In desperation, I reached out for salvation.

"Hey, Reggie, You got any weed?"

"This isn't Reggie. He's in jail."

"Okay. Thank you." *I guess I won't be eating the best carrots in the universe today.*

* * *

My cell phone was a constant source of frustration as well, and my relationship with it became mutually abusive. I admit to tossing it around a bit. There was something weird about the buttons. Sometimes they worked and sometimes they didn't, and it had so many features that I couldn't navigate any of them. I pressed a button and nothing happened, or I pushed one and all kinds of things happened, but I didn't know what happened. The phone was disrespectful and the cell phone company's customer service recording device was as well. That obnoxious machine cheerfully said "Goodbye," and hung up. Just like that. *No-o-o-o-o! Now I have to drive to the phone store and take a number to be abused and disrespected in person.*

At one point, my high-tech thermostat began showing temperature in Celsius instead of Fahrenheit. Bummer. I researched the problem online, which resulted in a technological gangbang mercifully relieved when *It* started hibernating and ended the madness. At that point both my thermostat *and* my computer didn't work.

Around the same time, the living room television suddenly went to black and white. A repairman resolved the problem.

He unplugged it and plugged it back in, a concept he described as re-booting.

The repairman said, "That'll be $85."

"Thank you."

I didn't have a good relationship with my GPS either. When planning a trip, I made the dealership set it up so I would not head out for Kansas City and end up in Waco. I learned the hard way that GPS is capable of giving directions that keep me off major highways in which case I end up maneuvering around farm equipment and motorcycles touring old Route 66 while cars speed by a few yards over on new Route 66. The dealership makes satellite radio selections for me as well.

"I'm driving to Iowa, and I want to go up the Kansas side." I said.

"Do you want to go up Highway 69 or 169?" the serviceman asked.

"I want to go to Iowa on the Kansas side."

"Okay. What do you want to listen to?"

"Jerry Jeff Walker, Vern Gosdin, and T. G. Sheppard."

"Good choices." (He lies. He is a child. He does not know these people.) "Do you want me to set up Blue Tooth?"

"No thanks. I've already spent a fortune on the dentist."

One day detailers left the moon roof cover open on my car. I pushed every button I could find to close it. That activity created a host of other problems, including interior lights permanently lit. This meant I had to drive around town looking like an all-night casino.

Finally, my eighty-five-year-old mother in the passenger seat reached up, slid the cover shut, and sat there smiling like a Cheshire cat who just coughed up a fur ball on my spot on the sofa. I decided to take advantage of Mom's mechanical aptitude and asked her, "Why don't you shut off the interior lights, smart ass?" And she did.

Shortly before I went to California where I experienced my life-changing breakdown, I surrendered. Royally ravaged by technology, I had reached my limit. Done, fried, and whipped, I accepted dinosaur status. In a tantrum, or what my grandmother would call a conniption fit, I unplugged *It*, all related devices, and a complex mass of wires and gadgets and relegated them to the garage floor. Afterward, I felt a peculiar sense of being free and trapped at the same time. And I cried.

Technology was out of my life. It was my window to the world, and that window was closed. It was a crippling loss in a long string of losses. The synergy of those casualties overtook me. Begrudgingly, I accepted my plight. I was not an idiot (I knew not to eat anything black in my oatmeal), but I simply could not wrap my mind around the digital world. There were too many whelms.

Technology spanked me. It's not possible to have moxie while being spanked by technology. The problem was, I couldn't have moxie without it either.

chapter 9

LOST CONNECTIONS

Prowling—it rained men,
until it didn't.

Over thirty-some years of being single, I like to think I accidentally found my boyfriends—just ran into them like when you spot in-season cherries in the grocery store. But the truth is, I hunted them down, as did most single women of the era.

Under the guise of *girls' night out* or the desire to *just dance*, we hit the local clubs and dance halls when we were between boyfriends. Monogamous relationships and career demands dampened this activity periodically, but off and on up through my early sixties I did my share of prowling. It was fun, except when it was not.

Prowling required connections with girlfriends on a common mission. Men were the spice of our exploits, and we girls bonded with each other in the throes of *the chase*. Compadres we were—run-around buddies on the hunt, each having the other's back. Just as important as the prowling, though, was the girl fun and the dance. We adopted the credo: Y*ou can never have too much fun.* And we danced our little hearts out.

I was thirty and newly single when my girlfriends and I prowled for the first time. It was the seventies and the disco era had just kicked in. People make fun of disco today like I make fun of macramé, but I loved it then, and I love it now. To me, it signifies excitement squared.

I had several run-around girlfriends who provided the support a single gal needed to go to clubs without a man. Although we ate up the environment and relished the fun of it, we rarely dated disco aficionados. An exception was one girlfriend who married a dancing disco dude and later wished she hadn't. Their wedding song was *Another One Bites the Dust*, which foretold her future accurately.

The first time I walked into a disco, a packed floor of dancers moved in unison to *The Bus Stop.* Hundreds of people, dressed to the nines, glided to and fro like waves ebbing and flowing on a beach. It was captivating. Soon the DJ played *It's Raining Men. Hallelujah*! and the real dancing began. I was hooked. It *was* raining men all right, and I had to get all over that.

I didn't know such beautiful men existed. Clean shaven except for mustaches, which were popular at the time, these men were a vision and quite a contrast to the men I'd been exposed to in my small town living. Decked out in leisure suits, leather shoes, gold jewelry, and silk shirts, they reflected urban sophistication.

To fit into this world, I had to get with the program. I took dancing lessons, adopted a hairdo representative of a nesting habitat, and put on platform shoes worthy of Fergie. It was during this time that I acquired my first pair of red high heels. In them I learned to execute moves that required dancing tights under wispy dresses. I adorned my hair with flowers and layered on enough makeup to be a circus performer. And I danced.

For several years after that, disco was very, very good to me. Donna Summers sang for the girls and the Bee Gees crooned it out for love. Although I rarely met anyone to date at a disco, I danced my way through some handsome dance partners. This was heavy stuff for a newly divorced country girl. Tulsa clubs revealed an urban world I never knew existed, and I liked it.

Two distinct types of people populated discos: the dancers and the partiers. Most serious dancers came out to dance and maybe drink. The partiers came out to drink and maybe dance. We dancers called the partiers amateurs because they couldn't dance so well, and they thought of us as amateurs because we drank water—lots of it. Drinkers were sloppy, sometimes even forgetting that a requirement for dancing is standing up. And they were not typically receptive to dancing advice, such as:

"Perhaps you should stop now."

"You should not spin."

"Dipping is not your thing. Get off of me."

I was dancing with a drunken fellow who spun around several times, wobbling like a top about to fall over. The man ended up several yards away dancing with someone else, and he didn't even realize it. His new partner looked at him as if she had just birthed a baby when she didn't know she was pregnant.

I could have retrieved the dancing tornado, but odds were he was going to spin again, and he didn't have enough redeeming qualities for me to chase him around the dance floor to *Disco Inferno*.

Run-around buddies, dance partners, and the disco crowd provided a tribe of sorts, people to hang with and have fun. With my intense focus on career, they were a valuable distraction. But this tribe, like so many, fit the times and when the times changed, it disbanded. Fortunately, another one took its place.

* * *

In the 1980s the Urban Cowboy movement invaded Tulsa clubs. The artificial sophistication of discos was replaced by smoky, down-to-earth dance halls full of both urban and real cowboys in hats, Wrangler jeans, and Roper boots. Although the ambiance attracted its share of country folks, the same faces that graced the discos also frequented the country night clubs. The crowds were playful, casual, irreverent, and congenial, except when a fight broke out.

Fights were frequent in country dance halls. Most of the country guys had been fighting all their lives. When one cowboy says to another, "You are going to need a bigger truck, asshole," a fight is pending, and it's time to leave. Someone is going to lose, and too many Oklahoma men have guns in their trucks, if not on their person.

Given my country background, the country ambiance fit me better than sophisticated discos. There are two types of country clubs: honky-tonks and dance halls. Honky-tonks are bars, usually with a small dance floor. A country dance hall has a huge dance floor, which facilitates the sweeping circular movement of the dance. Famous clubs are Billy Bob's in Dallas, Gilley's in Houston, and The Tumbleweed in Stillwater, Oklahoma.

The best dance hall in Tulsa is The Caravan. Spawned by the Urban Cowboy movement in the 1980's, it is still going strong today and attracts both urban cowboys who order steaks from the Internet and country folks from all around who butcher a cow from the field and put it in the freezer. Each dance hall has its own style of dancing, and out-of-towners can be spotted by their unique dancing style.

Country dancing is deeply ingrained in Oklahoma's culture. I know this because I was with a group touring McAlester prison on a project to study crime when prisoners yelled from their cells, "Can we dance with your women?" (They also said, "You sure do have purdy lips," which was directed at a fellow in our group who was too good looking to ever set foot in a prison—or a Tupperware party.)

Dance halls in Oklahoma are smoky. Rural Oklahomans hold on stubbornly to their smoke and chew. A haze fills the air and drifts around dancers like clouds, giving an ethereal feel to the atmosphere. If you want to participate in the dance, you suck it up and breathe the poison. My willingness to expose my lungs to these hazards reflects the degree of my infatuation with country dancing.

The first time I walked into a country dance hall, I was instantly smitten. It looked as though dancers were roller skating as they moved around in a large circle while managing somehow to spin and twirl at the same time. The motion had a frantic nature to it, but the faces of dancers reflected exuberance and frolicking fun. The twang of steel guitars, drone of fiddles, and nasal tones of singers lamenting cheatin' partners, trucks, prisons, rodeos, rain, whiskey, and hunting dogs added to the ambiance.

Soon dancers moved in unison, similar to disco line dancing, except they rotated in a circle and periodically yelled something that sounded like *Bull Shit.* Women yelled it, and no woman I knew would do such a thing. Was I hearing right?

I asked the man next to me, "What are they yelling?"

"They're yelling *Bull Shit!*"

"Well, *Bull Shit!* I have to do this."

"I'll teach you."

I found more boyfriends prowling in country dance halls than I did in discos, probably because of my propensity to gravitate to country boys. Over time, I learned to be discriminatory about which country boys to take up with. A girl could get burned, and sometimes it's better to stop, drop, and roll than to fan such a fire. I harbor a visual of me meeting a handsome man and then dropping to the floor and rolling around. Any man who doesn't run under this scenario is an idiot. However, there are men who are attracted to a crazy bitch. I just really don't want to be one.

A turning point occurred when I went out with a man who was an exceptional dancer but wound so tightly he could whip a grizzly. On the way home from our date, he peed in a ditch while I sat in his truck—a vehicle with one working headlight, a gun rack in the rear window, a lariat on the floorboard, cigarettes in the ashtray, and a bumper sticker that said "God, Guns, and Whiskey," I touched my finger to the bullet hole in the passenger window and concluded, *I need a boyfriend with a better truck.*

Heavy drinking is the norm at country dance halls. Keeping in mind that the goal was to find a man with a better truck, I fended off a fellow too young to have a nice truck and too hammered to have good sense. When he asked me to dance, like he could possibly manage to do so, I declined. "Well then, I guess fucking is out of the question," he slurred.

Most women would have been offended, but it struck me as funny. His eyes were glazed over (in a country bar, this is known as having your beer goggles on). He listed to one side and had that ridiculous upper body bounce drunks have while standing still. When his eyes rolled backward like cherries in a slot machine, which signaled he was about to fall over, I grabbed his shirt and steadied him.

In the state he was in, he was a harmless, cute little fellow, and he reminded me of my son who was in his early twenties and beginning to frequent dance halls. My motherly instincts kicked in, and I danced with him to keep him from falling down. He latched on, breathed in my ear, and hummed *Okie from Muskogee* to Alabama's love song, *Feels So Right.* One of his friends danced by and asked if he still lived with his mother.

When traveling, I checked out the country dance halls and was usually disappointed, especially on the East or West Coast. In California the men looked like Irish dancers, all pointy toed while dancing to *Bull Shit!* This was pig-snorting comical to someone from Oklahoma. It eliminated any prospect of the men being appealing. On the East Coast, country line dances were done to Barry Manilow's *Copa Cabana* instead of Brooks and Dunn's *Boot Scootin' Boogie*. This sight can cause an Oklahoma gal to laugh so hard that tears and snot dilute her Margarita. *Please stop. I can't take anymore. I'm going to die here.*

* * *

To go prowling, a girl must have a run-around buddy. This is someone worldly enough to know where to stand to get asked to dance and to not take a purse into a club. Sophisticated prowlers never ask a friend to guard their purse. Anything they can't get in their jean pockets is stored in their bra. If a man gets too close, he's going to wonder what kind of party is going on in there if the phone vibrates, but a girl must have her prowling supplies.

A run-around buddy relationship may be a temporary one based solely on the process of prowling, like my friendship with Pepper. Our relationship ended when she went to jail for embezzlement. However, a couple of run-around girlfriends turned into forever friends. Samantha is one of them. She and I looked so much alike that people assumed we were sisters. So we went with that and entertained men with a routine wherein we argued about which one was the younger sister. This was fun for the men until we asked them to guess which sister was older. The question created a dilemma—if they were sober. Impaired men don't have dilemmas until the next morning.

Another run-around buddy who became a forever friend is Cookie. She and I don't run around anymore, but we are still friends. She's married and I've mellowed, but we had a good run at partying well into our early sixties. Cookie is wickedly funny. She runs at full throttle and is capable of producing an "Oh shit!" moment in a heartbeat. I describe her as an "outlier," one of those unique, fun-loving people who sees the world differently than everyone else. That is what I love most about her.

Dr. Maya Angelou said, "Use moderation in all things, even moderation." Cookie moderates her moderation but little else. She believes you can never have too much fun, but we did occasionally have too much fun.

Most of our run-around time was spent at country dance halls in Tulsa where the regulars called us Frick and Frack. We distinguished ourselves by wearing heels with our jeans, more as a protective measure than a fashion statement. We didn't want to look so country that some guy might conclude we would get on a horse. If a cowboy suggested we would look *purdy* on his Appaloosa, we could say, "In these shoes, I don't think so."

Nothing is more gleeful than a two-stepping cowboy steering his woman through a crowded dance floor like NASCAR's Ricky Rudd working his way through the pack. The dance hall environment is complicated, though, especially for someone like Cookie. She served ten years in the Army, and she can be feisty. She told me once, "In the Army they don't teach you to fight. They teach you to kill."

Cookie could stare down a mad pit bull. No one in their right mind would mess with her, but not everyone in a honky-tonk is in their right mind. Knowing Cookie would throw down when challenged, I advised her up front that if she got into a fight, I *did not* have her back. She needed to know that. I trained at Toastmasters International. I was never in the army.

One night it happened. She got into a girl fight. A mean girl, with a fake ID and drunk as a rabid skunk, was unaware of dance hall protocol. She took Cookie's chair while she was dancing and wouldn't give it back. Cookie was going to get her chair back. I knew that. The regulars watching the situation unfold knew that. Cookie asked nicely at first. She usually starts out nice, but the mean girl introduced foul language and then did the unthinkable. She pushed Cookie.

Those of us who knew her had no time to hold our collective breaths. The mean girl hit the ground in an instant with a raving fifty-something mad woman on top of her with a death grip on her throat. Several of the girl's friends were all over Cookie, beating her and pulling her hair to no avail. They were like gnats to her. Cookie was focused, zeroed in, and she didn't let go until the bouncers got there to pry her loose.

I worried Cookie would be in trouble, but the mean girl survived Cookie's attack to kick a bouncer in the crotch and to resist a policeman trying to cuff her. When a law enforcement officer tells you to put your hands behind your back, you do so. It is not a good idea to hold up two index fingers and say "Don't touch me." You just don't do it.

The girl was soon yelling, "Get off of me." The next words she heard were, "Have a seat. Watch your head." As it shook out, the mean girl went to jail, and bad ass Cookie left with her date.

"Why didn't you help me?" she asked him.

"It looked like you were doing fine all by yourself," he said. "I was just disappointed there was no mud."

From then on, the guys at the dance hall called Cookie "Sugar Ray."

A fascinating parade of people frequented the honky-tonks. Cookie and I used to make fun of them, but we stopped. And for good reason. After she made mean-spirited comments about a cowgirl with her lips plumped up with so much filler that she looked like a sock monkey doll, Cookie had a raging cold sore on her lip the next morning. When we snickered about a girl in short shorts showing off a knee brace that could have easily been covered up with jeans, Cookie's knee hurt something awful the next day.

We learned our lesson, and from then on when we observed a target for ridicule, we didn't say anything. We just looked at each other and laughed. When a strange-postured guy danced by, looking as though he had a corncob up his butt, we laughed so hard we spewed beer, but we didn't say a thing. That posture wouldn't be attractive on either of us.

A hefty, hard-breathing fellow on the verge of a cardiac episode told us he came to Tulsa to dance because women in the dance hall in his hometown were fat. I asked Cookie, "Are you thinking what I'm thinking?" We didn't say anything, though. We weren't looking to gain weight. Cookie did tell the guy, "Fat girls shouldn't be a problem. A real cowboy could drink those women skinny."

A man (who was born on third base and thought he'd hit a triple) tried to impress us with his interest in world travel. When he referred to Guatemala as guacamole, we teared up. Our shoulders shook, and we choked on our Margaritas, but we didn't say anything. No one wants to get stupid.

Cookie and I took our Frick and Frack routine to a Dallas dance hall where a cowboy invited us to a gun show, so we invited him to a Mary Kay party. The next day we ran out of gas at a Dallas intersection in 107 degree heat. Still in our nightclub makeup, we stood under an overpass for shade, waiting for rescue. Young men in a passing car assumed we were working girls and offered us $20. We said, "TWENTY DOLLARS? Get the hell out of here."

At this moment, a cop pulled up. Fortunately, he was focused on the traffic situation, and we avoided going to jail for solicitation. I wanted to go into my *Thelma and Louise* routine where Cookie is the one who shot somebody and I suggest he tase her and take her to jail. He was excessively grumpy, though, probably having a bad day, so I went into my "yes, officer" routine instead.

Just in time, a handsome Texas gentleman cowboy in Wrangler jeans, boots, a starched shirt, and a silver belt buckle emblazoned with a longhorn motif stopped to help. I told him we were idiots because we ran out of gas. He said, "You're not idiots, darlin'. It could happen to anyone."

Well, if that didn't just make me feel better about the current problem and life in general. God knows I'm a sucker for a man who calls me darlin'.

After putting gas in the tank, he volunteered to follow us to a station down the road. With the cowboy trailing behind in his shiny black pickup truck all trimmed out in chrome accessories, I became unduly distracted by the sight in the rear view mirror and drove past the station. He flagged us over to tell us, and I again suggested we were idiots.

"I'm beginning to believe you're right," he said, and he drove off. The cowboy rode away. Just like that.

* * *

During those run-around years, I was mostly focused on country boys, but Cookie took up with bikers occasionally. Eventually, she sucked me into the vortex of motorcycle bars and biker rallies. I was shocked one day when she asked if I would stand up with her at her wedding. She'd been dating this biker dude for two weeks, but she often dated bikers, so I didn't think much about it.

Cookie knew I would think she was batshit crazy to be marrying someone she had known only a couple of weeks. So before she told me she was marrying Carl, she asked that I not yell at her. I had no urge to yell. I just wanted to know, "Who the hell is Carl?"

Cookie's actions sometimes suggest that she has lost her mind, but she experienced a health crisis shortly before meeting Carl. It forced her to stare death in the face, so she doesn't react to situations like the rest of us. But then, when I think about it, she never did. Marrying someone she had known for two weeks was Cookie just being Cookie.

She is a dear friend, so I agreed to stand up with her at her wedding at the Reformed Criminals' Biker Rally in Podunk, Oklahoma. I assumed the event would be attended by old criminals. Since I had never been to a biker rally and because I'd heard stories about them, I asked Cookie, "Will I be expected to show my titties there?" After that issue was resolved to my satisfaction, I inquired about safety. Cookie had already arranged security for me in the form of a biker dude named Dirty.

"You'll be safe with Dirty. No one would ever mess with him." This was comforting. Maybe.

"Can I call him Dirt for short?" I asked.

"I'll check on that. It's not a good idea to offend Dirty. That could ruin the wedding and possibly the rally."

Next, I learned I would not be walking down an aisle. Instead, I would ride in on a geezer glider up to a stage occupied by a band called *Whiskey Dick*. I thought perhaps a geezer glider was some kind of customized flatbed truck or something of that nature and that the experience would be similar to being in a parade. But Cookie explained that a Geezer Glider is an awesome motorcycle to be driven by a biker named Dog. It was there, on that stage, with *Whiskey Dick* in the background ready to play the wedding song, *Wild Thing*, that Cookie and Carl were to be married by a minister known as Drool.

Cookie decided I should meet Carl and her biker friends before the rally, so I found myself in a biker bar on a Tuesday night, probably overdressed and too polished off, but having a high old time with Cookie, Carl, Monk, Dunk, Dog, Dirty, Bad Brute, Fargo, some nameless man with missing front teeth and a hang-dog look that reminded me of an old dog named Rufus, and a couple of biker babes obviously not taking their medication. I felt as though I was in a band and was the only musician in it.

The festive group decided I needed a biker babe name. We settled on Doggie if I'm with Dog and Dusty if I'm with Dirty. I didn't anticipate any such conversion as I was unlikely to attach myself to a biker; however, sometimes I do things I shouldn't. An enlightening experience all around—I got a flavor of Cookie's world, and it was fun.

Carl, a dead ringer for Jon Bon Jovi with a bit of John Stewart mixed in and a touch of the better attributes of Mick Jagger, is a bit of a wild man, but he is solid. And he has a good heart. Most importantly, he is clearly crazy about my friend. They are together to this day.

After an evening at the biker bar and an episode of shopping for studded black leather pants for a wedding at a motorcycle venue, I faced the reality that perhaps my appreciation of diversity was a character flaw. Although exposure to the Tulsa motorcycle crowd revealed a surprisingly caring and benevolent culture, this was not my tribe. To integrate this venue I would at some point have to get on a Harley, and that was not going to happen.

My run-around buddy, Cookie, could always be counted on to draw me into experiences outside the cocoon of the ordinary. She was my spark. Although I can't say I found my tribe at a honky-tonk or a motorcycle event, I relish my times with her. As long as I don't get into a girl fight or take off on a motorcycle to the southern point of South America with a guy wearing an ankle device, it's all good.

Cookie got married as I retired in my mid-sixties. My prowling days were over. I still wanted to dance, but I had no run-around buddy, and I was no longer having fun. This was another loss in a string of losses that haunted me as I headed to California to help my daughter with her new baby and to collide with my internal demons.

* * *

When I retired, the severing of workplace connections was surprisingly swift, which is often the case. Then another tribe started falling apart. This tribe was formed many years ago by professional women who bonded while in graduate and law school. Together we raised children, earned degrees, and entered a wasteland devoid of female perspectives and lush with male egos—a business world representing a microcosm of a football game.

As professional women, we supported each other through the early career years and reveled in the accomplishments of the later ones. We met frequently for happy hour and breakfast. Two males usually joined us. We named our group *The Diva Consortium,* and we called our guys groupies. We had moxie. When you have groupies, you have moxie.

We were all there for each other. When boyfriends ran off, leaving us feeling like Ruby the dock whore, we rallied around. In the university years, one Diva tutored me through a calculus class, and I helped her with homework when she went through a divorce and couldn't concentrate enough to read. I knew what that was like. I couldn't concentrate for several months after my divorce and other breakups with Ronnie, and Blake, and Dakota, and Max, and Dillon, and Cooper, and Tanner and . . . I often got backed up on my reading.

Two friends and I were the core of this group. The groupies gave us the designations of Diva I, Diva II, and Diva III, the labels determined by boob size. I was Diva II. The Divas engaged in animated discussion regarding the ranking, but the groupies resolved the issue like referees at a hockey game, and who could argue with that. The boys knew their boobs.

Like most men, our groupies were preoccupied with breasts. I found this irritating because I tried to convince girlfriends not to expose cleavage at the office. It made them look as though they were too big for their dresses. Nora Ephron noted that as a woman ages certain areas of her body take on the appearance of peach pits, and cleavage is one of them. No one listened to me. This became a raging controversy, so finally *The Divas* surveyed our groupies at happy hour for their opinions. The boys endorsed cleavage, at any age, anytime, and anywhere.

"Surely, not at the office," I said.

"Oh, yes, yes, at the office is good," they said, nodding their heads enthusiastically like bobble head dolls.

One groupie qualified his endorsement, proposing that the amount of cleavage should be in direct proportion to the alcoholic consumption of the woman. "Four-finger cleavage is inappropriate on a drunken woman," he said.

To reinforce his point, he developed a sliding scale of the appropriate ratio of fingers to cleavage and alcohol consumption and recorded his conclusions on a napkin from Lou's Bistro. That involved three too many variables for me; however, a *Consortium* vote on his calculations sealed the deal, and I was so over asking the guys for input on cleavage. Sometimes the groupies were annoying.

The Divas occasionally rounded up our groupies for happy hour by promising wild sex or hinting that one of us was not wearing underwear. We never revealed which one, which made me feel like one of those nutshells in a magic trick. Of course, we never kept our promises, and they didn't expect us to. The spicy flavor of our conversations was intended simply to make us feel that we were sexy. And we were. We were fifty-something and in our prime.

Our groupies were generally useful, particularly as a source of the male perspective on important issues. We gave them quizzes from ladies' magazines and conducted roundtable discussions on such topics as: Would you date yourself?

They helped us understand that smart women want to be hot, and dumb women want to be smart. Their advice was usually right on, but I thought they missed on this one. Dumb women just want to have big boobs.

Since our groupies were businessmen, they put everything into business terms including romance. To determine if one of us should date a guy, the boys performed a *business analysis worthiness test*, which began with a pro forma projection on the prospects of a viable relationship. Data was gathered and analyzed. Then they listed the pros and cons, calculated the return on investment, considered opportunity costs, identified threats, contemplated the competition, and hypothesized about optimal outcomes.

After a breakup, they performed a residual value analysis and generated a lessons learned summary. When I dated a cowboy, they were quick to suggest a contingency plan. The Divas assisted them with their due diligence, and this explains why none of us ever successfully dated anyone.

Although taking advice from the groupies on personal matters was suspect, they were a binding force that assured that calmer minds prevailed among the willful Divas. We were counseled, consoled, and on one occasion mooned. One of them even helped save Diva I's life. She was choking on something at dinner. I patted her on the back. The groupie patted her on the chest. Which technique worked is unknown, but I rewarded our groupie by brushing crumbs onto his lap and then brushing them off. It was a mess. We all looked out for each other.

I went to Oklahoma City with Dwight, one of our groupies, to shop for furniture for his house. He drove and I discovered that it offended him when I pointed. This was a problem because he had never been to OKC, and I needed to steer him around. After noting his aversion to pointing, I tried to accommodate, but at a critical time, if I didn't point, we would be on the freeway to Wichita. So I pointed. Dwight griped—loudly, "Quit pointing. I hate that." *Oh no you didn't.*

I lost it. I gave up my weekend to keep him from mixing Victorian furniture with urban metro, putting up denim curtains in his bathroom, and purchasing a Batman bedspread, and he won't let me point? So I got my psycho freak on and said, "I will damn well point if I want to, and you can just fuck off!" The silence was thick as Dwight sat pensive for a moment contemplating the situation. Then he hit the steering wheel hard and said, "Well, fuck!"

It was again quiet for a few seconds. Both of us sat rigid in our seats. Suddenly we both started laughing. We laughed and laughed. Dwight pounded the wheel while not headed to Wichita, and I tried not to pee. From then on, I pointed and pointed, and he didn't say anything. Friends asked the next day how our trip went, and I said, "Well, we didn't go to Wichita, and I didn't pee in Dwight's BMW."

Like Cookie, Dwight is an "outlier." He is delightfully unique, and that is what I love about him. A high-energy person who can be impetuous, he runs in a higher gear than the rest of us. We went into furniture stores, ones I frequented often and where I had a reputation to protect. I warned the sales staff up front that my client had not taken his medication that day so they wouldn't be surprised when Dwight jumped on beds, although it's always somewhat of a shock to see a grown man do so even when forewarned.

It is a challenge to rein Dwight in, but he has a good heart. He is the only man I know who asks me what kind of music I want to hear when I get into his car. Until I met him, I thought that was beyond the realm of possibility. I've listened to my share of Boston, Kiss, ZZ Top, The Dead, Leon Russell, and worst of all, ranting and raving talk radio. Dwight delivered the slow jazz, soft rock, or classic country that I love.

I was just a couple of years into retirement when *The Diva Consortium* disbanded. Both groupies coupled up with wonderful women who somehow managed to accomplish the impossible and pass the *business analysis worthiness test*. Diva I moved to the mountains of Idaho, and Diva III began traveling extensively with her job. I was going to Iowa to help take care of Mom and to California to take care of a grandbaby with medical issues. So *The Consortium* transitioned into a state of rare reunions.

Without *The Diva Consortium* and my run-around buddies to shepherd me through my mid-sixties transition, I lost my anchor. Although losses of these vital connections took their toll, they were just a slice of the problems that forced me into a downward spiral. It was the menace of aging that pushed me over the edge.

chapter 10

THE AGING FAIRY
BITCH-SLAPPED ME—HARD

Body parts were moving around, downward mostly.
So I said, "Beat me, hurt me,
make me write bad checks,"
and my personal trainer tried to kill me.

I wished I weighed what I weighed when I first thought I was fat. Watching television one day I discovered I weighed more than Anderson Cooper—not just a little more, but way more. That's just wrong. He's not a big fellow, but he works out and is buffed up pretty good. A small-boned woman like myself should not top Anderson on the scales.

Perhaps I wasn't taking care of myself as well as I thought. I was taking all the proper supplements. I even took memory enhancing herbs; however, I only took half doses so I wouldn't remember everything. I didn't want to remember Hank. The problem was that for exercise I sat. When I felt good, I ate, and when I felt bad, I ate. I didn't allow vegetables in my kitchen because they got in my mouth, and I considered chocolate a fruit, and bacon a protein.

Something had to be done, but roadblocks held me back. One of them was exercise. It got the heart all churned up, and it was boring. On a treadmill while watching television, I was bored twice. So I did nothing—that was until a defining moment changed everything.

I had a boyfriend at the time (it could happen) who helped me squeeze my Size 12 body into a Size 8 bustier-type bra designed for a strapless evening gown. The bustier had the attributes of knights' armor, and it came down to a v-shape in the stomach area.

After my man hooked it in the back, I turned around to find him staring with shock and awe at a massive and strangely out of place v-shaped roll of fat on my belly that pooched out below the bustier. When he rallied enough to speak he said, "That's gonna show."

Desperate, I located a panty girdle and slipped it on over the bustier. This eliminated the belly roll but produced a significant roll of fat at the top of my thigh. The look of disbelief on my boyfriend's face reflected the mental reverberations stirring in his head. He declared again, "That's gonna show."

So I traded it for a long-line girdle, which caused a disturbing monumental roll of fat to materialize just above the knees. My boyfriend's eyes reflected alarm and panic— as though an arm suddenly stuck up out of a grave. Composing himself, he insisted I stop the madness. "If you go any further you'll have fat ankles," he said, "and there ain't no way to cover that up."

Future scenarios piled on layer after layer of never-ending physical degradation. The aging fairy, whom I thought had my back, bitch-slapped me—hard—over and over again. Ailments sabotaged physical activity and my metabolism went on sabbatical. Eventually, I decided to take on the mean-spirited fairy. I engaged in a fitness plan designed to give me the body of Catherine Zeta Jones.

Eating healthy is important, but I never do that, and thinking about it makes me hungry, and then there is that vegetable issue, so I focused my efforts on working out. Building strong bones and muscles and achieving balance were the primary goals. These qualities minimize the risk of falling and assure you can get up when you do. Otherwise, you might flail around until someone finds you. You can't have moxie if that happens.

Desperation is a serious motivator, so I walked into a training facility and announced, "I'm training for the Olympics. Beat me, hurt me, make me write bad checks." It is there that Levi, my personal trainer, tried to kill me.

I begged for mercy, "Don't hurt me, master. Please don't hurt me," which was futile. He handed me weights over twenty pounds each, and I dropped to the floor. Doing lunges down a hallway while holding weights in each hand, I begged people in the training rooms I passed, "Help me, help me." No one responded. They had their own "Oh, my god!" scenarios going on. Levi was not letting up, and it was clearly a matter of saving myself. So I threw up.

This sparked a new plan—jogging. Unfortunately, no matter how much I trained, I could only run for short distances. On Easter Sunday, breathless at the end of a short sprint in a park, I rounded the corner of a trail to discover a church congregation sitting on a knoll listening to a spirited sermon. With all those people watching me round the curve at a pretty good pace, looking like some kind of jock, I felt compelled to keep up the image. So I maintained the jog longer than I was conditioned to do.

A few yards down the path and out of sight of the congregation, I doubled over. Gasping for breath as bicyclists and joggers dodged me, I said my very own Easter prayer, "God, please let me live, and I'll never eat bacon again."

My intermittent efforts at fitness were misinterpreted by people at work. They assumed I was some kind of sporty person. Company promoters asked me to lead a team in the Tulsa Run. I said, "I don't run."

"That's not required," they replied. "We're participating in the Fun Run, and lots of people walk."

That was a lie.

The gun went off and everyone ran so, of course, I had to run. A mile down the road, I sat on the curb with my head between my legs promising to never eat bacon again. I prayed that I not barf in front of several hundred people, including workmates who ran by waving.

One of my employees sat down by me on the curb and patted my back. Not wanting to ruin her run, I begged her to go on, but she refused. So in between gasping breaths I promised, "Sarah, . . . when . . . I . . . get back . . . to . . . the office . . . on Monday . . . I will . . . give you . . . a raise."

Rallying, I started walking to the finish line with Sarah by my side, probably reviewing CPR protocol in her head. Crowds encouraged the runners and a group of high school cheerleaders began rah-rah-rahing me as I moped by. *You've got to be kidding. I'm dying here.* I wanted to yell back at them to "S-H-U-T U-P," but I didn't. Instead, I smiled, issued a weak wave, and threw up in my mouth.

Later that year, company promoters asked me to enter a corporate challenge in the flexibility category. I had learned my lesson, so I told them, "I'm not flexible."

"But they will put you in a category according to your age. You'll do fine," they said.

"I AM NOT FLEXIBLE."

Since workout plans were not going well, I considered that perhaps it was not so bad to weigh more than Anderson Cooper. Anyway, working out intruded too much into couch time where I backstroked to reach potato chips and fudge. I just needed to learn to love my tummy, which stuck out beyond my boobs and required that I wear maternity clothes from Target. When dancing, my partners and I bumped bellies, and I endured embarrassing pat downs when going through security. But, oh well.

The consequence of this line of thinking was predictable. I got way, way fatter than Anderson Cooper. Something had to be done or I would soon be Jabba the Hutt. People would beep when I back up. I would develop a preference for Velcro, elastic waistbands, and orthopedic shoes. I wouldn't be able to dance throughout *Louie, Louie.* So I again pursued a workout plan.

The degree of my desperation was reflected in the intensity of that plan. It included no less than three programs. (I'm not obsessive.) At a fitness center, I mounted an assortment of weight machines. For a woman my age, this was equivalent to climbing a fence with a shotgun. On the up side, I got to work out while watching myself in mirrors that made me look thinner than I was.

At a "women only" workout center, I did circuit training with my sisters while listening to songs by Cher and contemplating back fat, the world situation, and oatmeal, raisin, flaxseed, almond, no-sugar, gluten-free cookie recipes. Sometimes we talked about men and how when they do dishes they don't wipe off the counters.

To round out my workout, I did yoga to flute music, bubbling brooks, and chirping birds. It was there that I learned there is such a thing as a yoga accident. Against the advice of my instructor, I strapped ankle weights on my legs to intensify the workout. (I'm not obsessive.)

The first time I did so I lay on my back and lifted my legs up over my head. The ankle weights caused my feet to keep on going, striking Ed, the boxing dummy used to train you to punch from your core. The movement ended with an unintended backward somersault. My instructor looked as though she had just spotted ET. Just as surprised, and as wild-eyed as a kid who tasted his first pickle, I uttered a resounding "Wow!" I would have said, "I meant to do that," but I sensed she wouldn't believe me.

Even without weights, certain yoga positions made me wonky. I occasionally listed to the non-dominant side. If I were a man, the listing inclination would be determined by the direction of my comb-over. (I have no scientific data to support this premise, but I take every opportunity to discourage comb-overs wherever I find them.)

This valiant, three-pronged fitness approach failed. Ice cream and bacon sabotaged it, and I wasn't even close to getting a body like Catherine Zeta Jones.

This sparked a new plan, something less complicated and more doable—walking. Trudging by a house under construction in my neighborhood I noticed Hispanic bricklayers swarming all over the exterior. Loud, pounding music blared from their flatbed truck. Having once been a disco devotee, I started jerking my head sideways to the beat. Two workers sitting on the back of the truck noticed and began jerking their heads. By the time I passed the house, the workers on scaffolding around the house were side banging to the beat as well.

When I came by again, after completing my loop, someone turned the volume up, and we did it again. It is inspiring to have workout buddies, but bricklayers are not particularly mobile, so they were no good to me at all.

* * *

An active woman needs a man who is reasonably fit, at least one who can do downward dog without getting dizzy and who will not fall down while dancing, possibly taking her down with him.

One of my boyfriends was a *teeterer*. As a preemptive measure, I would grab him by the shirt and level him out when he started leaning, usually backward. I kept my elbow straight when doing so as he tended to latch on. If he managed to complete his fall, I preferred to extricate myself and avoid doing downward dog.

He fell to the floor once as dancers parted to give him space to roll around down there like a June bug on its back. I kicked him and told him to get up. To do so, he assumed the knee-chest position, which bump and grind enthusiasts call the spanking position. I didn't spank him, though. Such things have a way of coming back to bite you.

Eventually he worked his way back to a vertical stance by applying an old stripper move I taught him so we could both get up from getting a little bit lower when dancing to *Shout*. This required that he send his butt up first after which the rest would follow. Once recovered, my partner resumed dancing as if nothing happened. So did I.

Although I generally manage to remain standing while dancing, I do have awkward tendencies outside the norm, which make me prone to falling. People who know me well are not surprised when we are walking along and I suddenly disappear. They laugh, which is wrong. A baseball fan robustly called me "SAFE!" As I lay on a stair landing after rolling down fourteen steps, a skydiver friend complimented me on a great tuck and roll.

In another incident, while rushing down the hall of a movie theater to the restroom so as not to miss the ending of a movie, my toe caught on the patterned geometric commercial carpet. This sent my body out ahead of my feet. As I tried valiantly to catch up, my feet slapped noisily down the hall. This caught the attention of people in the lobby just as I came shooting out of the hallway to land on my belly at their feet. With all that racket, they surely expected some kid to come running out, not an old woman in mom jeans and orthopedic sandals.

People were so shocked that they just stood there in disbelief, popcorn and soda drinks in hand. Finally, the young fellow behind the concession counter leaned over and asked if I was hurt. Since I fall down a lot, I had my line ready. "No. I meant to do that."

I tinkled a bit when I hit the floor hard, but it was not necessary for him to know that. I managed to squirm around enough during my recovery to eradicate any puddle. I had a boyfriend at the time. (It could happen.) When I rejoined him in the movie theater, I couldn't stifle the giggles. He assumed I loved, loved, loved the ending of the movie. As we drove home, I was force to confess the incident when the smell of urine permeated the car causing him to ask, "Who peed?"

In another falling incident, I broke my arm. I wish I could say I did it working out, but I was really drunk on a boat. This required that I endure a cast on my right arm for six weeks. The experience taught me why a coyote chews off his foot when caught in a trap.

Frustrations built to a breaking point one morning when I struggled to put on panty hose (a dress code requirement for work). I cried and unleashed a string of severe sentence enhancers. I had a boyfriend at the time. (It could happen.) We were in the early honeymoon phase of the relationship when he gave a crap, so he tried to comfort me.

"What's wrong?" he asked.

"My whole body is falling apart."

"You're doing fine—getting better every day."

"What do you know? You have no idea what it is like to not be able to put on panty hose and to have your whole body falling apart. I bet when you turn sixty you'll have high blood pressure and you won't be able to eat salt."

He pondered that for a moment and then said, "You'll never know. Your whole body is falling apart. You'll be dead by then." Touché.

The broken arm took me out of commission for a while. Once workouts resumed, progress was modest, and I never did get the body of Catherine Zeta Jones.

Then the gods delivered shapewear. I became *The Price Is Right* excited when I found one with sleeves designed to slim the upper arms in addition to reining in tummy and back fat. A marvel it was.

This blessing turned on me, though. It was a hot summer day the first time I wore it. I broke a fingernail putting it on but was soon sashaying around at a picnic with slim arms and a flat tummy under a t-shirt that said "The older I get, the better I was." The problem revealed itself when I got home and tried to escape the constraint. Sweat had bonded every inch of that spandex straitjacket on me like skin on a seal. It would not come off.

I tried everything, but once that wonder garment got up around my shoulders and arm pits, with the sleeves still tightly stuck to the upper arms, it wasn't going anywhere. It was as though I'd been attacked by a tire tube.

Trapped in mounds of elastic stretched tightly across the shoulders, chest, and arms, I began to feel claustrophobic. The more I wrestled, twisted, and pulled the tighter the device felt. Panic set in. Back fat, underarm bulges, and globes of pleasure pooched out below the constraint as if they were water balloons about to burst. The scene would frighten any self-respecting fireman, so 911 was not an option. No one deserves to see that.

Finally, in an act of desperation, I located scissors and hacked my way out of that body shaping monster. When it snapped off, body parts burst out of the elastic mass like a dog who discovered someone left the gate open. I was suddenly several sizes larger with flappy arms and happy to be so. It was at this time that I determined shapewear was a sign of the decline of the fabric of society.

This was a turning point. I accepted that I weighed more than Anderson Cooper and probably always would, and I would never have the body of Catherine Zeta Fucking Jones. However, Levi was no longer beating me, I was not writing bad checks, I had bacon, and I could go *a little bit lower now* when dancing to *Shout* and get back up. I could also dance all the way through *Louie, Louie.* And occasionally, I even had a boyfriend. (It could happen.)

* * *

I tried viewing my body as a wonderland, but I wondered where certain parts went as they shifted around, downward mostly, and I wondered when they would stop working all together. Since I would rather fall into a vat of caramel than fall in love, I teetered on the edge of whether parts moving around was important or not.

Too much was required to look beautiful. I maxed out when I learned plastic surgeons recommend you sleep on your back. They could look at a woman's face and tell which side she slept on. This explained why when I woke up in the mornings my face looked like an unfortunate crochet project. I tried to sleep on my back, but I kept turning over in the night. Someone suggested I sew a tennis ball on the front of my pajamas. It would wake me up when I rolled over. Really? Really? Oh my god. Really? What if I die, and I'm discovered in bed with a tennis ball sewed to the front of my pajamas?

Discouraged, I continued to sleep on my face. I also withdrew from workouts entirely. *Why bother?* As a result, my posture deteriorated. This added another layer of concern. I worried my frame would end up so stooped that someday when I'm in a wheel chair, caretakers will have to strap me in to keep me from somersaulting out. I feared I would become one of those people who, when seen from behind, would appear to not have a head.

The aging fairy's betrayal and the state of my fitness weighed heavily on me, but I didn't have the energy or fortitude to do anything about it. My body was just another element of life that was not going well, and of those there were many. Together they mounted a fierce blitz that led to The California Crash.

chapter 11

INVISIBLE:
AT SIXTY YOU BEGIN
TO DISAPPEAR

The sting of dismissiveness.

Almost three, Bethany was becoming increasingly interested in being social, and she sought out people connections wherever she could find them. Sitting at a park concert in front of two elderly ladies in their seventies, she turned around to them and asked:

"What's your names?"

"I'm Vera, and this is Florence," Vera replied, delighted to be asked.

Next, Bethany asked a question familiar to her, "How old are you?" She expected the ladies to hold up fingers.

Surprised and tickled by the question, Vera answered, "I'm seventy-two. Florence is seventy."

"Oh," responded Bethany, who could count to twenty. She turned around, sat down in her chair, and thoughtfully pondered the mystery of Vera's answer. Shortly after, she scurried off to dance in the grass to a reggae beat, demonstrating moves that delighted Vera and Florence. With her long blond hair flying through twists and turns and some rather amazing bumps and grinds, she was a blaze of youthful glory—her whole life ahead of her.

Later, as the ladies were leaving, she said, "Nice to meet you." Not having yet learned that people like Vera and Florence are irrelevant, Bethany may have been the only person to interact with them at the park that day. In their seventies, they were in the realm of irrelevance—a stage of life that in our culture is viewed by most as a time when nothing matters. They were invisible.

* * *

After retiring in my sixties, I lost my professional identity —my edge. On the fringe of things instead of at the center, I was disappearing. My life was empty except for being a mother and grandmother, and my depression had begun to interfere with those roles.

I was no longer sitting at the lunch table with the cool kids. This feeling was reinforced often. While on a break at a women's meeting, I stood with three impressive young women engaged in spirited conversation. After several of my comments were ignored, I excused myself (with no one noticing) and joined another group where I had a similar experience. It was as though I wasn't even there. I was invisible. I didn't think much about it at the time. Later that evening, though, something was bothering me. I couldn't put my finger on it. Resurrecting memories of the day, it hit me—*the dismissiveness.* In the eyes of those young women, I was irrelevant.

Ann Landers described this situation when she said, "At age twenty we worry about what others think of us. At age forty, we don't care what they think of us. At age sixty, we discover they haven't been thinking of us at all."

It was wounding to be perceived as insignificant, but I accepted the dismissiveness of the exuberant young as the natural order of things. That acceptance didn't make my emerging role as a trivial player okay. With the robust years fading into the past and nothing to replace them, I was on a collision course with a serious funk.

* * *

The sting of dismissiveness from men all the years I worked added to my sensitivity to being considered irrelevant. No matter how competent I became, there were those who considered any rewards undeserved. They minimized everything I did. Successful programs were discounted or made fun of. Ridiculous male perceptions and double standards intruded in perplexing ways. If I talked at all, I talked too much in their opinion, while men pontificated all over the place.

The harsh aloneness in the workplace was almost crippling. I didn't fit in anywhere. Relationships with those above me were awkward. Relations with those below had to be arm's length out of necessity. Peers were mostly men. In their minds everyone was competing and everything was a game of one-upmanship. I didn't think like that. This isolation fed my sensitivity to being trivialized.

I was buoyed when other women were brought into the higher ranks of the company. However, connections with them were restricted. A cliquish *good-old-girl* network would have been professional suicide, and we women knew it. So we tiptoed around the male persona so as not to be threatening. With personal connections with women limited, their presence did little to reduce my isolation.

* * *

Once I retired, challenges at work were traded for problems from another source. Growing old is a harsh master, and the angry truth of that was soon revealed. A barrage of signals announced my irrelevance and foretold a catalogue of future provocations and losses. Although I was introduced to the reality of growing old while in my early sixties, the distraction of work suppressed any reaction for a while. Retirement was the game changer that brought aging to the forefront, and I began to flounder in a negative sixty-something mentality.

As bad as that was, even deeper influences gnawed at me. Lost love finally did me in. I could no longer love wide open, and I decided I'd rather live the rest of my life alone than ever hurt from a relationship again. Love was a mistake. Even the Dalai Lama said, "Love is the absence of judgment." So romance was off the agenda.

Although I pined over the loss of love, a smoldering contempt for romantic prospects intruded. When love songs came on the radio, I changed channels. The last thing I wanted was to see a movie or to read a book about a love story. When friends fell in love, I grappled with cynicism about things working out for them. I found fault with any man who tried to pierce my bubble. One said that to date me was like chasing a gnat—probably not an overstatement. Although I appeared to be hard enough to roller skate on, underneath that exterior was a fragile girl too damaged and emotionally vulnerable to embrace love. Backing away from it increased my isolation.

While all this was going on, a number of scary things happened. Misfortune was unrelenting. Trying to be strong for those around me, I became more and more vulnerable as every ounce of my being was directed at saving newborn grandbabies. As one rallied, another one was born with life-threatening issues. Smoothing processes for anguished parents and comforting suffering babies was all consuming. For two years, I was mentally tortured by their struggles and taunted by the fear of an outcome of which no one could speak.

The babies rallied, and participating in that should have made me feel relevant, but the accomplishments were overshadowed. They introduced a level of dread I had never known. Fear of the future haunted me. How could I bear something bad happening to a child we invested so much into saving? The burden of apprehension ate at me.

Other family crises hovered. The anguish of nursing my dying mother swallowed me up and foreshadowed my own future. Then, at forty-four, my son suffered a frightening widow maker heart attack. He survived, but that rocked my world in the worst way. How could I cope with the loss of a child? Three of my brothers had been felled by heart disease, which compounded my fears. I became concerned about my fate and that of other family members.

Then, just when I thought I couldn't take any more, the recession hit and jeopardized the financial security I took for granted. Suddenly, I faced the prospect of someday being poor and a burden to my children. I interpreted this as an outcome worse than dying—the worst-case scenario.

Then the final kicker. The inability to master technology crushed my writing dreams and devastated my self-esteem. All my life I had been a *can do* gal. Now I was an incompetent failure. My computer sat on the floor of the garage while I wondered how it could irritate me so much just sitting there. I was free of it, but it teased me as I grieved the loss of my dream. I knew it was my window to the world. When that window closed, I was shut in.

The exodus of run-around buddies from my life as they made their own adjustments to aging added to the sense of loss. I wasn't having fun anymore.

With all these pressures, I abandoned enlightenment. It was as though I didn't have the strength to take in anything new. All my life I was a seeker, but after retirement, learning faded into the background as a looming depression brewed. Seduced by the perception of what aging is supposed to be like—an *I've worked and paid my dues* mentality—I nestled inside my bubble. I dropped out.

I no longer watched the news as it was disturbing. I avoided the polarizing subject of politics. I read moronic books and magazines and watched mindless television shows, all of which made me uninteresting. I turned into one of those old people who tell the same old stories over and over again because nothing is going on in the present. I was just existing. No wonder I was disappearing.

* * *

When I headed to California to help my daughter with her newborn baby, my red high heels were stored in a box in a closet. Wearing them didn't feel right anymore. With the halcyon days behind me, I had evolved into an old woman—a befuddled misfit. A line in the book *The Kite Runner* describes what retirement was like for me at that time. I had been "lifted from the certainty of turmoil and dropped into the turmoil of uncertainty."

My age became the most important thing about me, and I had no strategy to deal with it. I interpreted the concepts of *young at heart* and *sixty is the new fifty* as silly. Unlike friends, I had no interest in the test that might determine that a person's biological age is less than their chronological one. (One friend took the test when he was sixty-four. It revealed that his biological age was eighty-one.) I preferred to face growing old head on, but I didn't know how to do so in a positive way.

A consummate realist, I determined that how old you are is how many years you've lived. That *is* your age. Period. My pragmatic nature, which was aligned with this concept, was not the problem, though. It was that I allowed the negatives of aging to overwhelm me while I ignored the opportunities. I failed to realize that when something is lost, something else is gained.

Giving in to the status of a maladapted dinosaur being hammered into extinction, I became a negative spirit. Although I lived well, there was an absence of passion and purpose. I treaded water. Moments of bliss so common in the past never happened. Unlike many retired people, I didn't have a bucket list. I had an anti-bucket list composed of things I never wanted to do again. This was an expansive shift from the younger, upbeat me. The strange, raw world I had created was disorienting. In it I lost my moxie. And I began to become invisible.

Life took on the attributes of a bad karaoke moment where things are not going well, but the singer feels an obligation to finish the song anyway. I didn't know I could just stop, that I could change. I accepted my plight, but my world was gray, and I was tired—tired of me.

All aspects of my life were a mess and looming issues fought in my head like battles raging on multiple fronts. Anguished, I became a phony—acting happy while resigned to complacency. If there was a theme that described my life, it would have been a mournful "My life has come to this." I needed a lifeline, and The California Crash, as traumatic as it was, threw me that line by launching a rally that changed everything.

I watched my willful three-year-old granddaughter hold her position with her older brother, insisting that if she was to give up her baby doll play to be a pirate, she got to have two swords. Finally, he acquiesced after which she declared "Aaarghhh!" and tore after him waving both weapons with a vengeance as he ran like a drug dealer on COPS.

Her dad said, "That girl is going to be trouble." He was right. She demonstrated some serious moxie, and she was a girl after my own heart. With an eye patch and two swords, this sweet, gentle little princess with jewelry and a tutu under her pirate gear became indisputably relevant, a gal to be reckoned with. I thought to myself, *I want some of that. I want my moxie back.*

—THE RALLY—

RED HEELS
AND SMOKIN'

chapter 12

RELEVANCE:
GETTING THE MOXIE BACK

Refusing to disappear:
At sixty-something, I could easily have
thirty-some years left—one-third of a lifetime.
That's a lot of time to waste.
Once wasted, it is time I can't get back.

When I had moxie and a man made an inappropriate come-on, I responded, "In your wildest dreams," an alternative to pepper spray. When a pest assured me he'd be right back, I said, "Don't threaten me." When someone at work put me down, I studied more, worked harder, and ran circles around them. When a guy mooned me, I told him he had pimples on his butt, which caused him to check it out in a mirror. When opportunity showed up, I struck. I took strategic risks and made gutsy moves. I felt within me a sense of bravado. I wanted to be that plucky woman again —the one who had moxie. I wanted to refuse to disappear. I wanted to feel like wearing red heels again. So I studied, I explored, and I learned a better way to be in the world.

Although aging is the omnipresence, it is a privilege—one not everyone gets. Growing old is not so much about the body as it is about the mind. Such revelations suggested a shift in core assumptions from the ones that drove the negative interpretation of my life that led to my bad behavior in California.

When I left there in an uncharacteristic overreaction, I was forced to deal with the circumstances and conclusions that caused me to float in nothingness. I might have endured that state for the rest of my life had it not been for the incident with my daughter and her grace following it.

Disturbed by the unhappiness I tried to ignore—and to hide—she steered me into therapy. "Please, Mom, go see Dr. Amy." Like the child searching for a toy who said, "It is very somewhere," I knew my moxie was "very somewhere," and I desperately needed to find it. So off I went to therapy.

Dr. Amy hands out *peace of mind* like candy. A clever, accomplished woman, she is one of the smartest, most intuitive people I've ever known. This petite spitfire with copper hair and searching eyes possesses a contrasting mother-earth quality that is endearing and comforting. Empowered with exceptional analytical skills and a focused approach, she gets to the heart of a matter quickly. She was just what I needed to instigate a rally.

Although we had never met, I was no stranger to Dr. Amy when I showed up for my first visit. I had discovered her years ago when seeking pre-marital counseling for my children, and I referred friends to her. So she operated on the fringe of my world and was the ideal person to navigate me through my inventory of issues, of which I had prepared a list—in detail. (I'm not obsessive.)

As I revealed my litany of problems, she listened intently, made notes, and nodded as if to say, "I hear you." When finished, I summed up my predicament. "I feel disoriented. It's as though I'm shopping for bath oil in a farm equipment store. Something is off."

Dr. Amy took in the onslaught and ferreted out how I got into such a desperate state. She noted that the world had not been kind. I had been slammed. This explained my train wreck and made me feel normal. I was not an unhinged, bonkers old woman after all. Reassurance that I had justification for how I felt was soothing. I began to exhale. *Great—some peace of mind.*

While articulating my problems, I made disparaging remarks about myself. Dr. Amy was having none of that. She said, "I know too many people who know you to believe the image you're portraying."

Whoa. Dr. Amy dished out a direct hit. She didn't literally say I was full of crap, but she got that point across and set to work with her compassionate, no-nonsense approach. Picking up on my embarrassment at being in such a state, she cleared up a concern. "Your state of mind is not a sign of weakness. It is a sign of having been strong for too long." *Nice. More peace of mind.*

Dr. Amy explained that I was being incredibly normal for someone in this stage of life—another comforting thought —and I wallowed in *peace of mind.*

My issues were not uncommon among people my age. Two years into retirement, I was on schedule for a crash. Therapists are often sought out a few years after people quit working. Retirees initially relish the release from the severe structure and rigorous obligations of jobs, some for the rest of their lives. Others slip into melancholy as I did. Not having a passion did not suit my obsessive nature.

After just a few sessions and some homework assignments, Dr. Amy proposed a three-step treatment plan—a rather unorthodox one, I thought:

>-Buy an *Apple* computer and support package.
>-Decorate the house for Christmas.
>-Go to church.

I was troubled by her plan. I had no confidence any expedition into the world of technology would have a good outcome, and I harbored no enthusiasm for Christmas. Unfortunate experiences with churches predisposed me to disregard the third suggestion. So only out of desperation did I execute her treatment plan.

Technology had inhibited two vital aspects of my life: connecting with others and realizing dreams of writing. So I focused on that first and bought an *Apple* laptop and the support package, which included one-on-one training. I mastered technology enough to communicate with others and was soon on the path to writing my first book. This was huge.

Taking on the second step, I decorated my house for Christmas. The introduction of lights and sparkle into my space lifted my spirits. They reminded me of a happier time when I put lights all over my canopy bed and surprised my boyfriend when I pushed the twinkle button at just the right time. Holiday decorations set me on a path to nesting—a nurturing process that had always fed my spirit. Some ornaments yielded a troublesome legacy of glitter, though. The last time I saw that much glitter, a cowboy had gotten too close to a stripper.

Dr. Amy knew I needed a tribe, and she knew where I could find one. Before broaching the third step, she looked at me hesitantly, and I guessed what was coming.

"You are *not* going to tell me to go to church," I said.

"Yes, I am."

"It won't help. I did that and there was too much judgment, prejudice, and right fighting. I felt bullied."

Dr. Amy suggested a Unitarian Church. She said, "There is no creed. No one will tell you what to believe. Religious authority comes from within yourself. All religions are embraced. The focus is on service and love."

Over the years, I struggled with the inability to buy into everything a church expected me to believe. Some of it I could accept; a lot I could not. Yet, I was expected to believe all of what someone else told me was "the truth." Their truth didn't make sense to me. I'm too much of a pragmatic realist and independent, rational thinker to blindly engage in group think. Also, I require separation of church and *hate*. I was surprised when Dr. Amy's counsel proved to be right on. I found my tribe at a Unitarian church, and I found the path to service and love.

Dr. Amy's three-step plan worked. Over the course of the next few weeks, she and I teamed up and conquered the issues dancing around in my head, with one exception. We never resolved the romance hurdles. She didn't give up on them—I did. I wasn't ready. Dr. Amy told me to come back when I was ready. I was never ready, and I didn't go back.

* * *

A valuable lesson came out of this whole messy California experience. It is important to my children and people who care about me that I be okay. When I am not, I create burdens for them. My daughter knew I was not okay. A mental void did not suit me, and she saw that even when I did not. My fading vitality and despair cut her deeply. Facing that truth, I realized I had to do better for her sake and for that of other important people in my life.

Until my daughter picked up on my state of mind, no one noticed I needed rescue. The situation reminded me of an occasion when I was on a boat that was stalled in the middle of a lake and taking on water. My friends and I waved at passing boaters who enthusiastically waved back and went on their merry way. I felt like that while in my funk. Other people were cheerfully going about their lives while I drowned, and no one noticed.

This was my fault. I hid the despair that manifested itself in melancholy, thereby sabotaging any opportunity for rescue. Then I overheard my daughter's conversation with her friend. Their words revealed that my despair was made transparent by my frame of mind. Awareness of how I made them feel sparked the defining moment that changed everything. Their pity for me and the dread of their own futures shocked me into reality.

As I began to reshape my future I realized I could easily have thirty years left, one-third of a lifetime. This was something I hadn't thought about before. My future was a monster blank slate on which to write.

Free of the encumbrances of earlier years, this should be my time, my best time. Wasted, those are years I can't get back—one-third of my life spent as a victim and showing others this persecuted state is what being older is about. I didn't want that to be my legacy. I had to get my moxie back, so I fashioned an affirmation:

I will not be a victim—ever—no matter what happens. I will not waste the years I have left torturing myself or others with my issues. I will own my aging experience and view it as a privilege. I will live each day in gratefulness and make this last trimester my best time. I will be relevant. I will create a positive legacy by how I live.

With this affirmation, I became determined not to miss out on the woman I was meant to be. I confronted nonsensical political rhetoric. I began to fight like a girl again, to speak out on women's issues—more loudly and fervently than ever. I challenged younger women to do so as well. I even advised my two-year-old granddaughter not to sympathize with her brother who was in timeout for hitting her.

I no longer shared minor problems with my children or others. When my coffee group talked about aches and pains, I changed the subject with, "Speaking of sex . . ." Still, I knew that if a major medical problem surfaced, I would have the good grace to share that misfortune and allow others to support my struggle.

Resolved to show how magnificent being old can be, I became inebriated with gratefulness for each day and the opportunity to make it count for something. But just aging well was not enough. I wanted to go *beyond* aging well, to make my aging experience an example for generations. So I pursued learning opportunities, which opened up my world.

I found a path to mastering technology and chased writing dreams. I wrote my memoirs and filled them with lessons learned and spirited adventures. I shared that learning with others by developing seminar programs on capturing life stories and aging beyond well, which I offer to groups and organizations. I was creating *legacy squared.*

With a feeling of relevance back in my life, a newfound sense of adventure flourished, and I became brave about having fun. I sought connections and found new tribes. A range of possibilities flourished and a renewed zest for life emerged.

With the weight of depression lifted, I reveled more freely in the blessings of spirited grandchildren. These splendid creatures rocked my world with artful creations made with macaroni and countless possibilities for mattering. I conspired with them to hide peas in glasses of milk and thanked a little fellow who shared an impressive booger by putting it on my breakfast plate.

When I travel to California to visit *Thing I* and *Thing II*, my suitcase is loaded with toys. Their mom has instructed *The Things* that it is not polite to ask GoGo for toys immediately upon her arrival, so when I get there, they are restless with pent up anticipation and hopefulness.

Although generous with urgent greetings, they are no doubt happier about the arrival of my suitcase than myself. They squirm and fidget, gaze at it longingly, touch it, tap it, and circle it, their eyes pleading for that which they cannot ask for outright. I torture them briefly while harvesting hugs and kisses and then cave in to their torment. The eruption of gleefulness and happy, hopping feet when I begin to unzip my bag stirs such a commotion of blissfulness in me that the question of why I'm pushing seventy and still here is answered. I am the toy fairy.

Grandparenting introduces a new level of setting an example. For me, this is somewhat disconcerting because I can be a tad too irreverent. I portray violent fights between Easter bunnies (someone has to die), and sometimes I swear. This has earned me the reputation in my family as "crazy old Aunt Nik," alias Grandma GoGo, the one everyone warns the children about.

I go to California regularly to visit *The Things*. A girlfriend reminds me to be careful at the beach because life guards don't try as hard for old ladies. This is not a problem as I rarely go to the beach. I have other motives for my trip. People I sit next to on planes ask why I'm going there. I say, "To get my hair done." This is not entirely untrue. I do get my hair done in California by Caroline.

She works in a shop full of beautiful California girls. The stylists and customers wear high heeled shoes and trendy clothes. Fabulous hair and movie star figures with remarkable cleavage abound. In comparison, my Size 12 self could be classified as a hog, but I have California hair.

The last time I was there a woman on a bike had a wreck and sat in front of the windows of the salon nursing an elevated foot. No one paid much attention until the police showed up—hunky men who looked like movie stars. The salon energized as hairstylists and customers checked them out. The girls began arguing as they staked claims on the beautiful men.

Then an ambulance pulled up, introducing medics who looked like Paul Newman and Robert Redford in their heyday. The salon virtually erupted when the men exited the vehicle and the claim-staking accelerated.

There were not enough men to go around, and the women turned on each other. Knowing such men were out of the range of possibilities for me, I sat in Caroline's stylist chair with foils on one-half of my head bleaching me platinum while she distracted herself with the irresistible attraction of adorable men. Then a firetruck pulled up.

The salon hushed as the women waited for the exodus of hunks from the truck, and they were not disappointed. Several gorgeous firemen came into view and the girls celebrated each one. Arguments resumed. The last man out of the truck was an older man, sporting an impressive bald spot and a beer belly. *Possibilities*. I staked my claim. "He's mine," I said. No one protested.

Caroline decided to take bottles of water to the rescuers. The girls stood at the windows oohing and awing as they watched Caroline strut around, flip her luscious hair, and deliver sustenance to our men. Finally, she turned to return to her post (where I sat wondering what happens to hair after the platinum stage and whether I would look good in one of those styles where one side of the head is shaved). The poor injured woman interrupted her exit and asked if she could have some water, too. Caroline realized her omission and obliged.

As I sat among the beautiful people, I felt strangely *out of place* and *in my place* at the same time. This is because I had my moxie back. Regardless of what happened around me or what anyone else thought, I mattered. I was part of the fun and living in the moment. I was relevant.

* * *

Fortunately, Dr. Amy and I pulled my life together just before Mom died, and I was able to work my way through that loss without losing ground. As I observed Mom's final days, lessons were revealed that I might have missed before my newfound sense of relevance. I grasped the significance of how a person deals with the end of life. That process leaves a mark, and it can be good or bad.

As a tribute to Mom, I became even more determined to live in a way that creates legacy and to do dying well—to the extent that I can control the process. And I reaffirmed the promise I made after Dad's death years ago, to live my life in a way that returns his investment in me.

Mom's last months were difficult, so I focused my memories on the good times we had before the end devastated her so completely. Some of my favorites were of the many road trips we took together. It was not uncommon for us to be stopped by the highway patrol. While I viewed an opportunity to interact with law enforcers as an adventure extraordinaire, Mom never acclimated to the experience and was traumatized the second the blue lights started flashing.

With her Iowa farm woman persona—short, round, white hair, calico print dress, and old-fashioned glasses—she bore a stark resemblance to Mrs. Santa Claus. When pulled over one day, I rolled down the window, pointed to my passenger, and told the patrolman, "She made me do it."

He leaned over to observe Mom's body frozen in a statue-like facade. With hands in her lap holding a handkerchief and a purse hanging from her arm like Queen Elizabeth, she had grandma written all over her. Once the officer had a chance to take that in, I requested, "Would you please take her to jail?" I whispered, "You know, she kidnapped me." I got a sense he wasn't convinced, so I took my defense to a higher level and admitted, "We are *Thelma and Louise*, and *she* is the one who shot somebody."

He called my bluff and said, "Ma'am, I would take her to jail but I would have to tase her first." This produced an unpleasant visual in my mind.

After he presented me with a warning ticket, he noted that my passenger looked suspicious and was surely a threat to any community. We were ordered to continue on to Missouri and to not make any stops along the way.

As I pondered the many memories with Mom and Dad, the degree to which a person is relevant was driven home. I became even more determined not to fade into the background and vowed to make my life count. For an older person, though, relevance does not come easy. You must fight for it. An old folk tale illustrates this vividly.

Two elderly women were abandoned by their tribe in the snowy wilderness of the polar region. They were devoted grandmothers, and the tribe loved them, but children were dying of starvation and caring for the old ladies had become a burden. If children were to be saved, the women must be abandoned. The tribe wandered off into the frozen wilderness in a quest for food, tearfully leaving them behind in the bleakness of the snow-covered terrain.

Assessing their predicament, the women switched into survival mode and surprised themselves with their capabilities. They resurrected skills taught by their fathers years ago, relocated to a better site, and constructed shelter from the elements. They set about trapping and fishing and eventually amassed a substantial store of food.

In their nomadic quest, the tribe—still starving and ravaged by the harsh winter—stumbled upon the old women. Tribe members were shocked and delighted to find them still alive. The women, whom the tribe previously deemed an untenable burden, gleefully shared the rewards of their labors and rescued them all.

One might interpret the moral of this story to be that the tribe should have valued these elderly women more, but a deeper message exists. The women should have valued themselves more. They underestimated their ability to contribute and became victims dependent on others. Failing to realize what they had to offer, they deprived the tribe of their wisdom and talents. When the old women finally became relevant, it was not because of what anyone else did. It was because of what they did.

* * *

At sixty, one does not have to disappear. Doing so is a choice. Growing old is a formidable process, so it is easy to overlook the benefits, but wrinkles don't hurt, and old people are forgiven much. They can feed grandchildren marshmallows for breakfast and tell their mother they had fruit. They can be a hero, a rock, a source of adventure, or a profound doofus and children will believe they are somehow cosmically important. When you get really old, people begin to see you as cute, ornery, and quaint.

When something is lost, something else is gained. Free of the naiveté of youth and the burdens of childrearing and career building, older folks are exempt from many of life's encumbrances. They can do almost anything and not get tased or thrown in jail.

Even being in a wheelchair has benefits. You only have to iron the front of your dresses, you can pre-board in the throes of the airport caste system, and you can zoom, zoom, zoom as long as you don't treat people like bowling pins. By leaning into age, a beautiful thing happens—legacy.

As I broadened my perspective and enhanced my self-concept, age ceased to be the most important thing about me. I no longer looked at my life as if it were happening to someone else. Most importantly, I realized how much my life mattered. I got all over the aging thing. This meant it was showtime.

My rally was a matter of the mind. It required a shift in core assumptions and the adoption of more buoyant perspectives. I embraced those notions, pursued fresh interpretations, and discovered that age has the potential to be a tremendous asset. All I had to do to tap into that was to live in a way that inspires others and avoids creating burdens for them.

I began living in a state of gratefulness. Each day, hour, and minute became a blessing. I repeated my affirmation every morning, faced my issues head on, and found the diamond in each one. Many of them resolved on their own when my attitude changed. They just faded away like a dissipating fog. Immediately life was better. Other issues required work, but I was up for it.

I dug the red heels out of a box in the closet. It took a while before I felt like wearing them again. I had some healing to do. But just observing them in the closet nestled in a row of more modest footwear was nourishing. They reminded me of the vibrant, gutsy woman I once was, the one I would become again, one different from my younger self, but one who was smokin'—still.

chapter 13

LOVE: A FINE, FANCIFUL FRENZY—OR NOT

Lost love leaves a tattoo on the heart, but
Rumi said, "The wound is the place
where the light enters you."
So light me up. Well, maybe not.
Yes, do. No, don't. Well, maybe . . .

I didn't understand men any better at sixty-five than I did at sixteen, so I fell off my unicorn. Here's the problem. Every man possesses the qualities necessary to effectively mess with a woman. This behavior is innate as evidenced by a young boy, my grandson, who displayed the attributes of a charming, sweet talkin' dude long before his time.

At the age of three, the boy developed an obsession with handcuffs that came with his sheriff's outfit. I had invited people over for a social, and as they arrived he greeted them at the door and asked, "Why are you doing here?"

After the interrogation, he handcuffed them to the entryway stair railing. Later he handcuffed them to each other. This involved some novel connections, which spiced up the party. Eventually, a metamorphosis took place. The little guy became less hostile and not so much into bondage. Instead, he transitioned into a charming ladykiller. Throughout the course of the party, he indiscriminately and zealously acquired a number of girlfriends similar in age to his grandmother.

When Eloise, a lady in her seventies, was leaving, he escorted her to the door and inquired if they could get together Wednesday. (That was the day of the week his mother planned fun kid activities—his favorite day—so it was on his mind.)

Eloise agreed to the date, and as she descended the stairs from the porch, he waved and reminded her, "Don't forget about Wednesday." As she exited the gate, he yelled, "See you Wednesday." He was still waving enthusiastically as Eloise entered her car.

Men can be persistent like that, but Wednesday never comes—or it does, and they become gum in your hair.

That's not the worst of it. Men can be brazen and vulgar. When I suggested a guy put a bandage over the boil on his butt, he asked me to be more specific. Men don't fight fair either. I say, "Damn you," and they say, "You're welcome." These behaviors cause me to over-react and conclude that chocolate comes from a tree so it must be a fruit, and I eat some. Then I have to embrace a workout program to offset the calories. That makes my heart run amok so a cardiologist looks at my test results and says to his partner, "Are you thinking what I'm thinking?" Men can really mess you up.

In a vulnerable emotional state after the California incident, I didn't have the fortitude to face the truth of my romantic choices, so I tabled the love issues while Dr. Amy and I focused on other areas of my redemption. This was admittedly a cop out, but as my life had begun to blossom again in other areas, I didn't want to slow the momentum with the complicated, weighty nuances of romance. This was my healing time, and I didn't need that distraction.

It seemed like a moot issue anyway. I had concluded that love was a double-edged sword that was serrated, so I didn't have the fortitude to deal with experiencing it again. My defenses were up, and when I saw an attractive man, I immediately determined he was an asshole. In earlier years, when I was still the asshole whisperer, I would have found such a man attractive. Today, not so much.

* * *

The root of the problem was that I had made a number of poor love choices, which resulted in relationships that started as raging fires and ended as sterile and lifeless as computer graphics in a romance novel. This was because I built fantasies around men, and I settled when I should have said, "You are *not,* I said *not,* digging a grave in *my* back yard with a backhoe just to bury a dead raccoon."

Like most women, I took on the role of the asshole whisperer several times. I should have known that Captain Oblivious was not a good match when he picked me up for a dinner date and asked "What are you all dressed up for?" It should have been obvious that the need to advise a man to not drink and dress was foreshadowing. And, lordy, couldn't I have seen that an unconcealed gun on a date had asshole written all over it? Then there was the guy who hit a deer with his van and loaded it into the back seat only to discover it wasn't dead.

It's not hard to see the problem. I picked incompatible men who complicated my life. I could no longer listen to Aretha Franklin or Tina Turner while dusting. Television would be blaring out an action movie, football game, NASCAR race, UFO conspiracy film, Big Foot scientific documentary, or Loch Ness monster feature story, and the guy would have the gall to make fun of me for watching *The Home and Garden Channel*.

My tendency to rescue was also a relationship wrecker. I was susceptible to men who needed a break or who got a bad one—the *bless your heart* fellows. I would leave them a better man and find myself a devastated woman. Rescue is a man's job. No man feels good about being rescued, and as soon as he's saved, he will seek his own rescue project just to make himself feel whole again.

Realizing this, I gave up the rescue madness. Now when that *bless your heart* obsession sweeps over me, I run. When a man suggested I blow into his breathalyzer so he could drive, I held court with my common sense and released him into his natural habitat.

* * *

The unavailability of potential partners once I was in my sixties made relationship issues inconsequential anyway. Quality men were scarce. The reason was twofold. My fierce independence was hard on men, which limited the pool, and sharp men in their sixties could land a younger woman. This meant that to have a man, I had to either take up with one old enough that I qualified as a younger woman or take whatever I could get. Either option required settling. I did some of that in the past and my appetite for it had faded.

A five-year-old asked his father, "When I get married do I get to pick a wife or do I have to take what I get and not throw a fit?" Dad was stunned and perplexed by the question until Mom explained. When a kid complains at preschool that someone else got more macaroni than he did, he is told, "Take what you get and don't throw a fit."

I didn't want to take what I could get, nor did I want to throw a fit, so I disengaged. (The old platitude that "when you stop looking, it will happen" is overrated.) I moved out of the pet me and I'll purr stage, and it no longer did any good for a man to throw chocolate at me. I was done.

* * *

Even though I stopped seeking my next man to blame and avoided love connections after The Crash, I made progress on healing. I got all Kumbaya and accepted apologies I never got, and I took responsibility for my role in unfortunate romantic outcomes.

I did this by getting brave and participating in a relationship recovery program. It was humbling at my age to have to resort to such an action, but observing the dilemmas of the younger people in the group helped me realize that at least I was not the idiot I once was. Still, I had a lot to learn.

I learned that it is not necessary for either partner to make the other one wrong in order to break up. People should just break up. And I learned that the most important thing in a relationship is how each person makes the other one feel. Nothing else matters as much as that. This explained a lot.

If you make a man feel interesting, sexy, strong, and vibrant and he makes you feel the same way, you've got what it takes to make it. Fortunately, wine also does that. And so does chocolate.

Everything about love is good—until it isn't. Anytime a partner in a relationship doesn't make the other person feel good, the door is open for someone else to do so. As the relationship sours, it becomes an excuse for bad behavior. In turn, this provides justification for one or both partners to seek a new love interest. I now know how to recognize that situation. A girlfriend of mine put an Oklahoma twist on this. She explained:

"If your gut tells you something is not right, your guy is probably eyeing a new filly. He may not have ridden her yet, but he has most likely cut her out of the herd and picked out a saddle."

Most men prefer that the woman be responsible for the breakup and they employ a popular tactic, perhaps subconsciously, to get her to assume that role. They challenge her non-negotiables. If a man cares about his woman, he tries to please her. When he introduces behaviors he knows she cannot tolerate, he's done. On two occasions, when other women were waiting in the wings, a scraggly Grizzly Adams beard and a sudden passion for cigars (my non-negotiables) signaled that my men wanted out. I accommodated them both times.

Because it is common for a man to anger his woman so she initiates the breakup, I'm always suspicious when a man says, "She kicked me out." She probably did, but why?

In the relationship recovery program, I moved past some bitterness when I understood that men have their own set of vulnerabilities. They bear the burdens of masculinity. It must be hard to be susceptible to coy women bearing casseroles, desperate femmes fatales in need of rescue, turbulence-inducing drama queens, and boobs. Then there is the fact that women talk. Who needs that?

Women can be sassy. My six-year-old grandson admonished his younger sister for telling a lie. She responded, "You are not the boss of me. You are not big. And you don't even have a wallet." He will have to deal with such audacity from women the rest of his life. You gotta give it to the boys for putting up with us.

In general, the men in my life acted in a way natural to their gender. Their behavior was inherently different from that of the typical female counterpart. This proclivity is obvious even in small children. When I was on the phone with *Thing I* and *Thing II*, my two-year-old granddaughter gave me a long, soft, breathless Marilyn Monroe-esque "Hi-i-i-i-i-i." Her four-year-old brother took a clue from his sister's single-word conversation and said "Poop!"

Such innate tendencies don't diminish with age. Old men hit me, chase me with bugs, pull my ponytail, and scare me with loud noises. Such behavior is annoying, but I know they do it because they like me. This is sweet in a sense, but it doesn't make me want to bake them a casserole.

* * *

As part of my rally, I analyzed how I coped with abandonments and discovered that I created *faux fractures,* which are made-up victim stories about the breakups. My hurt didn't come from what happened. It came from the stories I created about what happened. My partners, no doubt, made up entirely different stories in their heads to justify their behavior.

Facts exist without human mental interpretation. Facts are what they are. Events are facts. Actions are facts. Conversely, stories are made-up thoughts created in our heads about those facts and events. They can be whatever we want them to be. We believe them no matter how far removed they may be from reality, just like the person who believes a distorted political spin or the man who decides that gravy is a beverage.

We do this because these thoughts suit our purposes and help us feel better about our behavior. Stories are designed to minimize a persons's role is a breakup and thereby reduce guilt, especially if they are the dumper. The person being dumped often makes up stories that fostered a victim status. I did that a couple of times. Thus I invented *faux fractures* that deepened the wounds.

My issues were not between me and my lovers. They were between me and myself. It wasn't what happened to me that made the romantic losses so difficult. It was the stories I created about what happened. These tales fueled my misery and made it difficult to move on.

When people showed me who they really were, and I didn't believe them or chose not to act on that information, it was my error. As Dr. Phil says, "You teach people how to treat you." This revelation helped me take responsibility for my role in the breakups, which was healing. He also often asks, "Do you want to be right or do you want to be happy?" Mucking round in crazy right-fighting thoughts won't make a person happy. Political spin is not real, and gravy is not a beverage. Believing otherwise creates fear and hate or fat and heartburn, and these outcomes do not lead to happiness.

A relationship either works or it does not. When things weren't working, I did nothing, which is the same as saying, "Mmmmm. Give me some more of that." Failing to realize that commitment is no longer required when a partner shuts down, I made the choice to do nothing. This set the stage for betrayal and abandonment. And who can blame a fellow for seeking happiness?

* * *

I'm still not back on my unicorn. The damage is deep. The last time I had a boyfriend, I cried when we made love. Poor guy. The tattoos on my heart remain and probably always will, but pain is a teacher and love a siren. Syrupy, fanciful thoughts still occasionally creep into my mind.

I fantasize about a connection so wonderful that I watch my man saunter in a manly way in my direction and the essence of him stirs me. But I'm afraid love will set off a commotion in my heart and then fade away, or I'll follow my pattern and choose an incompatible mate. We will be dancing at a wedding, and he'll drop to the floor and do the gator, which is not such a bad thing, but he may also describe a hard rain as like a bull pissing on a flat rock. Or he will tell my girlfriends he jacked up his truck because fat girls can't climb. Or . . .

When I'm tempted to spit on a man to see if he sizzles, I recall the hurts and disappointments of the past. It's not so much that I don't trust men; I don't trust love. Lost love has become a menacing shadow, and I wonder if I'm capable of opening my heart again. My guard is up.

Expectations are dim. I relate to a dejected Steve Martin when he said, "You know that look that women get when they want to have sex? Me neither."

Fortunately, Dr. Amy set me on a path of creating a life so rich without the love component that seeking it is not as all consuming as it once was. I'm open, but tentative. And I'm picky. It takes a really, really good man to be better than being alone.

I'm not the only one who has drawn this conclusion. Many of my friends, both men and women, have taken love off the agenda. Not all of them, though. A lady in her seventies who faced a serious medical condition was asked if there was anything she wanted to do while she was still able. She said, "Dear God, just give me one more boyfriend."

I occasionally have that thought, but I worry things won't go well and I'll drunk dial, make drive-bys, pine over lost love, create *faux fractures,* or other ridiculous behaviors people display when in the throes of the insanity of love.

* * *

The probability of love happening is buffeted by strong, unfavorable currents of the norm, so I hover in the crevices of romance. There, I set about proving what I already believe—that love won't happen. This is not difficult to do. Rather than get my freak on and pursue love or contemplate the void of it, I focus on nurturing friendships with men.

Perhaps love is afforded too much scrutiny. Friendship allows for a cadence of evolution that is less contrived. This approach has brought me out of a Garbo-esque retreat. Life in the periphery of love is rich with marvelous men.

We socialize without obligations or complications, mostly in coed packs. I wrote about one such relationship:

> A discussion group sat in a circle while the leader set the tone with an introduction designed to inspire robust conversation. Debbie entered late, looking good in fitted jeans and stylish pumps in a garnet red color that matched her scarf. Her look had casual sophistication written all over it. Darren followed her stride intensely with a look of immense pride—rather glowing—as if he were admiring something fabulous he had created.
>
> He is a champion of women and Debbie is someone he holds in high esteem, a woman he admires and respects. I noticed this because it is unusual for a man to view a woman this way— nothing sexual or territorial, just reverence for a classy, accomplished woman with whom he feels honored to have a connection. This suggests a capacity for friendships with women.
>
> Darren, a seventy-something intellectual, is like this with other women, myself included. Ours is a refreshing relationship, rich with engrossing discourse, which is easy for him because of his abundance of intellect and curiosity while challenging for me because I can only hope to function on his level.
>
> Possessing a virtual wealth of information on every topic imaginable, he is the guy you want on your Trivial Pursuit team. This makes it remarkable that he makes me feel as if I am in some manner fascinating, and I occasionally surprise him with more intellect or insight than either of us expects.

We have coffee with our irreverent, spirited friend Phoebe. She is what I call an "outlier," a delightfully unique person who possesses qualities the rest of us wish we had and the courage to express them. Every occasion is a meet-and-greet in her mind. Like me, it is easy to get her game-show excited, and she has energy to spare. Phoebe rarely says, "Yes." She says, "Absolutely!"

She and I have verbal filters that began failing at sixty, and neither of us is skilled at editing what comes out of our mouths. Depending on the level of culture and self-righteousness of our audience, we can be entertaining or annoying. We are fine with either one. Together we can be synergistically annoying, which is almost more fun than anything.

Phoebe is capable of casino rage, and she may tell someone, man or woman, that they have the testicles of a warthog, whatever that means. But she is also a soft and sensitive gal who believes the purpose of bread is to feed ducks. She messes with me, sending me texts when I'm sitting next to her that say, "I am sitting next to you."

I suspect some consider Darren, Phoebe, and me an odd trio and wonder what the connection is. It is simple for Phoebe and me. Darren makes us feel good. In friendship, as in love, it is all about how you make each other feel. A man who holds you in high regard, values your thoughts, champions your aspirations, and believes you are infinitely amusing is rare and addictive.

* * *

Love is a tempting mistress. As other areas of my life came together, I began to move out of the hermit mode. The prospect of dating introduced considerable trepidation, though. I was like a child confronted with a plate full of vegetables. One of my girlfriends tried to be helpful.

"The problem is penises," she said. "Every man is at one with his penis. It's a survival thing. Haven't you noticed that the expression on a man's face when he wants sex is the same as when he looks at biscuits and gravy? Just think, girlfriend, we could have just fed those men all those years."

That wasn't helpful, and I continue to harbor a residue of apprehension. I wonder if I would find love and then become nonessential—again. I wonder if the risk of a menacing loss will ever be less than the risk of love. I wonder if I will ever see another man so delicious that I want to taste him. I wonder if I can ever trust a man, relax into him, and put my being in his hands. I wonder if I will ever be thick with love or if it is something that was once, never to be again—an echo not heard. I wonder if I am constitutionally unable to love. I wonder.

I haven't climbed back onto my unicorn, but wounds have healed and life has a new texture. My happiness begins with me. Everyone else is off the hook. I view love as a fine, fanciful frenzy, and I realize I wouldn't trade any of my past loves for anything—except perhaps a Jaguar.

Perhaps I will meet a man someday who makes me think *I couldn't dream this big.* As I inch my way from remote possibilities to reasonable probabilities, I see love as something that was, is, and always will be achievable if sought in earnest.

I also know the tempest of it has ruined me, forever perhaps. If someone lights my fire again, I will team up with Dr. Amy in order to maintain my orienting axis. Otherwise, fear-induced sabotage would surely destroy faith in the process of love's evolution, and I would dress the guy in camouflage and send him for a walk in the woods so he would disappear.

* * *

Whether or not romance flares again is strangely unimportant at this point. Love does not always come in the form of a man. I love my life, and a love interest has the potential to mess that up. If I do dabble in it again, I've learned some things about senior dating that give me an edge. I know to get up early for breakfast dates so I don't have sheet marks on my face. I know that when I see young people humping each other on the dance floor that I should tell my date up front, "We won't be doing that."

I went out with friends one night who followed a band around town. We were a bit out of our element in an unfortunate club that reminded me of a prison visiting room. There, a man with missing teeth, clearly on his own unicorn, approached me and said I was prettier than a can of pork and beans. *Seriously? Who died and left me on the menu for meth addicts?*

Not understanding that "no" is a complete sentence, he clung to me like a tree frog until one of my guy friends asked him, "What part of *no* do you not understand?" With a single upper front tooth, the fellow reminded me of a can opener. If I went camping, he might come in handy. But I don't go camping.

chapter 14

FINDING A TRIBE

Everything in life is about balance.
You can do too little or too much of anything,
but you can never have too much fun.

You can't have moxie if you are not having fun. When I went to see Dr. Amy, I wasn't having any. To have fun, you need connections, and I was disengaged. As part of my rally, it was important that I find a tribe, or better yet, several of them. I did that. One of those tribes was discovered at church where I was surprised to find an irreverent, festive, intelligent, insightful group of people with whom to engage in stimulating conversation and fun.

One of these friends handed me a liquor flask when I arrived at church one day. Someone gave it to me at a gift exchange the night before, and I forgot to take it home. I'm not much of a drinker outside of social situations and for sure not one to carry liquor around with me, so I tried to give it away to my church friends. I was not successful, so I put it in the collection plate during the service.

As the plate passed down the row, one by one my friends spotted the flask and struggled to stifle giggles. When the usher spotted it, a perplexed expression crossed his face. I wanted to take a peek at the faces of surprised parishioners as the plate passed down the row behind us, but the potential disapproval of the usher and giving myself away held me back. Desperate to control our laughter, my friends and I froze facing the altar. Our shoulders bounced up and down from muffled giggles as we dug in purses for tissues and crossed our legs.

The next Sunday, I participated in a discussion group engaged in conversation about bouncing back from adversity. Someone commented about a flask dropped in the collection plate the previous Sunday. I froze. The group speculated on the reason and settled on someone pledging to stop drinking. My friends and I searched for tissues and crossed our legs. No one gave me away. The support of such friends was a big switch from the void I was in before Dr. Amy's plan pushed me to seek connections.

It is not unusual for people in my tribe to be on the verge of having too much fun. It's not all just about fun, though. We champion each other in large and small ways. I received a text from one of the girls that inspired me to lend support.

"It's 10:00 in the morning, and I've already consumed 1,200 calories."

To encourage her, I confessed, "I ate three ice cream cones last night."

"My glucose level must be through the ceiling," she said.

"Yeah, well, we're still Unitarians, though, aren't we?"

She and I are out-of-control women ravaged by bony-ass twits in television commercials and on display in magazines at grocery store checkout counters. These Hollywood women heckle us while we purchase bacon. We fat girls try to keep up by line dancing three times a week. The problem is that afterward we go to Rib Crib.

My Unitarian tribe helps me deal with many issues. This group is particularly important because the connections I had before I retired dissolved—just when I needed them most. Cookie got married, work friendships faded, and friends scattered around the country as they retired. And people died.

* * *

Dr. Amy easily identified the loss of connections as one of the primary reasons for my funk. Her recommendation to go to church was intended to encourage bonding, and it did the trick. Several tribes, large and small, were formed from this affiliation.

How these tribes came into being is simple. I put myself out there. In addition to joining a church, I participated in a singles group, a dance group, a writers' club, and a Friday night supper club. At these venues, I collected people. In packs, my friends and I participate in educational, fitness, and social functions. This bonding was easy to accomplish because other people needed a tribe as much as I did.

Connections really took hold when a friend and I started meeting in the mornings for coffee. We invited others and soon we had a good-sized coed coffee group meeting regularly at a place where everyone knows our names. We started out like the old farmers in small town cafes who contemplate the world situation and rib each other about one thing or another, but we transformed into more than that. We became a support group.

Such relationships are fueled by the void of romance, which is common in my age group. Participants are mostly unattached and available. These social connections are nurturing and insanely powerful. I miss my tribes when I travel, and those relationships call me home.

* * *

Another tribe was formed by accident—it evolved. I was out of town so much with Mom's end-of-life care in Iowa and with grandbaby medical treatments in California that I struggled to keep in touch with Oklahoma girlfriends. So I invited six of them over for an evening to catch up. We decided to do it again. Soon we were meeting regularly.

Since we were avid readers, conversation centered around books, so we named ourselves *The Girls' Book Club*. Other girlfriends were invited, and the group quickly doubled in size. Word spread and soon we broke twenty, not long after that thirty, then forty. With such a big crowd, we spent less time on books and more on lively conversation, so we became *The Unbook Club and Salon*. Since some fine grapes gave up their lives for wine, we drank some and eventually added *saloon* to our moniker. *The Unbook Club Salon and Saloon* was born, and my home became a clubhouse of sorts.

Before each meeting, we announced a discussion topic and selected a book we were *not* going to read. Still, some focus on books remained. The girls read poems and excerpts from their favorites: *The Flat Belly Diet, It Looked Good on the Model*, and *Does This Ponytail Make My Butt Look Big.* (No one would call us a serious literary group.) However, mostly we talked about such things as the fall purses at Target, Urban Decay's makeup line that stays on about as long as a tattoo, and postmenopausal zest. We exchanged purses, jewelry, and clothes. Every April, we dressed in vintage clothes, hats, and gloves for an annual English *low* tea party (high tea is above us).

Soon after the *Unbook Club Salon and Saloon* started, it became a topic of conversation at social gatherings. Men became unduly curious about our meetings and wrangled for invitations. "You need a rooster at those hen parties," one harped over and over. We could not allow men to invade our salon and saloon. No way. And we told them so in no uncertain terms. This intensified their interest.

"What do you talk about?" they pestered.

"Girl stuff," we responded, which further sparked curiosity.

Any mention of our meetings fueled their intrigue. I don't know what kind of girl stuff they imagined, but it must have been tantalizing because they badgered us relentlessly for details. Finally, I gave them what they wanted. "We talk about sex, blow jobs in particular."

The guys went nuts. My response was not a total untruth. We did talk about sex occasionally. A woman recounted searching for a man's junk under his big belly, a process that epitomized the saying "There must be a pony in there somewhere." Another revealed that she baked a penis cookie for a Dirty Santa party only to discover too late that the gifts were nice items. I admitted that I named my vibrator Sam Elliott. Of course, we would never share such stories with our men friends, particularly that we named our vibrators. But we did. Big mistake. The men have been beside themselves ever since.

* * *

I tend to gravitate to irreverent, down-to-earth people. On a cruise ship, I was bored with uppity provincial northeastern folks when at a disco one night I heard a Texas woman yell "Whiskey!" I knew then that I'd found my clan. Because of a rural Iowa upbringing, I don't relate well to the social set. No one would classify me as a proper, refined woman. I am more like unrefined white trash with some money.

I never did acquire furs or jewelry, which I view as dead animals and rocks. This makes perfect sense to me because that is what they really are. I have a deep, conceptual understanding of manipulation through branding and marketing, so people's fascination with brand names, chandeliers, and ridiculously expensive art is a mystery to me. I'm more likely to attend a ballet to see men in tights than to participate in any kind of cultural revelation, although I appreciate the kick-ass talent and artistry involved in the dance.

When I mingled on the fringes of the social set, I did so only because of business requirements and my connection with The Divas and other socially engaged girlfriends who eat goose liver pâté, drink chablis, and make fun of me for drinking white zinfandel. These right and proper folks would never use sentence enhancers, name a vibrator (at least as far as I know), nor would they bake a penis cookie.

They are unlikely to laugh at a liquor flask in a collection plate either, but they have their own approach to fun.

Social people are very much into gossip, multiple homes, luxury cars, collecting, and world travel. Gossip isn't even on my radar. I consider a second home or car a nuisance. Painted toe nails are my jewelry. Collections smother me, and possessions clutter my home. I once lived in a fine house and drove a luxury car, but those indulgences have no appeal for me anymore.

I can be talked into international trips by girlfriends, but I go only to share the experience. When my up-town friends talk about travel to the Greek Islands, Dubai, Paris, Singapore, or St. Petersburg, I tell them about my trip to Sapulpa, Oklahoma or the Chouteau Amish bakery. I make no apologies for my rough edges, and my girlfriends tolerate my anti-social proclivity with good humor.

When I mix with the socially elite, I sometimes think, *I gave up cowboys for this?* The activities of this crowd are incongruent with my personal life, and these social connections have produced awkward experiences.

To stimulate conversation at a right and proper party with my social friends, the host had each person draw a question out of a hat. My question was, "What did you get for Christmas?" I dated a cowboy at the time who gave me a steer horn belt buckle and homemade deer jerky, so I said I got jewelry and he cooked for me.

I have mastered maneuvering through such social situations pretty well, but I'm just a country girl who is only moderately successful at editing what I say. This old joke reflects my social inhibitions:

Betty Lou: "My husband bought me a Tiffany necklace."

Dottie Mae: "H-o-w n-i-c-e. My husband is building me a spectacular mansion."

Betty Lou: "H-o-w n-i-c-e."

Marg: "My husband sent me to charm school."

Betty Lou and Dottie Mae (in unison): "H-o-w n-i-c-e."

Betty Lou: "Why did he do that?"

Marg: "So I would learn how to say 'H-o-w n-i-c-e' when I mean 'Fuck you.'"

Like Marg, I occasionally say a drawn out "H-o-w n-i-c-e," when I mean "Fuck you." However, unlike my social friends, I'm capable of actually saying "Fuck you."

This joke circulated among my friends, and on a trip to Florida my girlfriend told a store clerk that we were celebrating our fifty-year class reunion. The young clerk seemed impressed and said that her ten-year reunion was coming up. My girlfriend said, "H-o-w n-i-c-e." The girl said, "Hey, I heard that joke."

In earlier years when we were out of graduate school and starting our careers, my socially connected professional girlfriends and I were anxious achievers, most of us single and raising children. Over time, we became empty nesting professional women living the good life, traveling the world, floating from man to man and perhaps job to job and even city to city. We maintained our connections until retirements and lifestyle changes loosened those ties. Also, my mid-sixties funk caused me to withdraw from socialization, so the frequency of interactions decreased and relationships lost momentum.

Since The Crash, I've come to appreciate the value of enduring friendships, and I reach out more. My friends and I have introduced fresh dimensions to our relationships and redefined our connections within the framework of our new retirement lifestyles. We take trips together, stand together in crises, and celebrate life's milestones. We are a tribe. The ties are now strong and enduring.

* * *

Once I reached out, I re-connected with another tribe formed in the 1970s when we were young married couples. Now, forty-some years later, we have become divorced or widowed, and we renewed our friendship. One of the men in the group had plenty of money and a reputation for being tight with it. So I tried my darnedest to get some. My efforts entertained the group. I worked him over pretty good, but all I ever got were some peacock feathers and a ride on his lawn mower.

So when another guy in the group announced that he expected a settlement from a lawsuit, I switched gears and went after him. "How much money are you going to get, Ray?" The next time we got together Ray had electrical tape wrapped around his wallet.

Since progress with Ray was stymied by electrical tape, I switched my focus to Grant. When he announced that he had bought more land, I asked, "How much land you got, Grant?" So far I haven't gotten any money or land out of any of them, although I'm still trying.

* * *

Another tribe is made up of two married couples and me. We were neighbors when we first bonded years ago. After getting smashed at a homeowners association party, we crawled to the nearest house to recuperate and have been getting together ever since.

I was coupled up with an asshole at the time. Fortunately, he bonded with another asshole in the group. (It is not pretty when assholes don't get along.) We should have called our group *Two Assholes and Four Nice People*, but we adopted the moniker *Five Gentiles and a Jew*. Since I no longer have an asshole, we are now *Four Gentiles and a Jew*. These folks are pranksters, and I try to keep up. I do this with yard ornaments: alligators, roadrunners, pink flamingos, etc. They got even once by telling my mother I was a lesbian, which was ineffective because Mom thought a lesbian was someone from the Middle East.

* * *

These tribes fit nicely into my third trimester experience. The most enduring connections, though, are with my forever tribe, which is composed of high school girlfriends. Although we are spread out all over the country, we take trips together. While planning our forty-year class reunion, the loss of a classmate caused us to decide to quit talking about doing something together and actually do it. As a result, we are closer now than we were as young girls when immaturity complicated relationships.

We took a road trip together up the coast of California. In the vicinity of the Hearst Mansion, we found ourselves at a roadside store late at night in a quest for food. It was there that we encountered law enforcement—a patrolman and sheriff's deputy in for coffee. They were handsome in their uniforms, badges, hats, and all those weapons, holsters, handcuffs, stun guns, flashlights, and radio gear. We were enchantingly festive, or so we thought, and struck up a conversation. This included educating the officers on the fact that Iowa stands for *Idiots Out Wandering Around.* We asked if they would like to hear one of our high school cheers. They agreed, somewhat hesitantly.

> A bottle of Coke, a big banana,
> We're from southern Indiana.
> That's a lie, that's a bluff,
> We're from Prescott, that's the stuff!

Everyone in the store seemed fascinated, especially since when we did the Indiana part we stuck our thumbs in our armpits and our elbows out for emphasis, just like we did in high school. Indications were that the officers particularly enjoyed the hand action on the big banana part. We ended with a maneuver somewhat reminiscent of a jump with splits, at least as close to it as women our age could get within the constraints of the grocery racks, lotto machine, newspaper stand, popcorn machine, and ATM.

Although the officers were in a state of shock, along with a store clerk and several patrons, we asked if they wanted to hear our school song. Someone said, "No," but the officers seemed up for it, so we did it anyway. There was no holding us back now. We belted out *Beer, Beer for Old Prescott High* with gusto, which caused one of the officers to ask if we had been drinking. I responded, "We ain't got no-o-o-o wine coolers."

It was obvious we needed a distraction from the drinking thing, so I asked, "If I laid down on the sidewalk outside, would you draw around me with that there chalk you guys carry around with you?"

This horrified my friends who dragged me away, concerned that the officers might interpret the lie-down-on-the-sidewalk suggestion as solicitation.

My girlfriends are medicine, and they are so fabulous that sometimes I feel how Mick Jagger must have felt when he had to follow James Brown in concert or the speaker who had to follow Martin Luther King's "I Had a Dream" speech. A diverse collection of remarkable, colorful, marvelous sisters, they royally entertain and sustain me even when I am one hot mess. Then there are my incredible guy friends. They are the frosting—chocolate frosting with nuts and coconut in it that conceals a tender, warm center.

These people are my tribe. We take care of each other, we share, and we have fun. You can never have too much fun, except when you ask a frogman on Monterey Beach if you can borrow his wetsuit for glamour shots because you don't look good in a swimsuit anymore, and he is not wearing anything underneath.

chapter 15

PERHAPS I LOOK BETTER FROM THE BACK

How to have game—or not.

When someone says, "You have nice eyebrows," it is a strong indication you don't have much else going on. Some women brag that they can still wear their high school prom dresses. I brag that I can still wear the same earrings. A lot has gone downhill. Parts have moved around—downward mostly. Years ago this would have bothered me, but not so much today. If I'm looking good or in style these days, it is mostly unintentional.

My son informed me that my new tennis shoes were trendy skateboarding shoes, which was news to me. I advised him, "I don't skateboard." Workout clothes encourage a workout, but skateboarding shoes don't make me want to skateboard. Nothing makes me want to skateboard.

Historically, what I looked like was a priority, and I was diligent about primping. Sometimes that preoccupation backfired like when I took a business trip with four men. Our flight was delayed, and we spent most of the day in airports. We arrived at our hotel thirty minutes before the restaurant closed, so we agreed to dump our luggage in our rooms and rush down to eat.

In my room, I noticed that I looked haggard. With little time to freshen up, I limited primping to lipstick and blush. In a rush, I used lipstick for both and put a stripe of bright red lipstick on each cheek and then on my lips. Using a small compact, I couldn't see the stripes on my cheeks once the lips were done and failed to blend them in.

Oblivious, I got on the hotel elevator looking like Geronimo. A man stared at me so intently that in my ignorance I concluded he wanted me. By the time we hit the lobby all indications were that he r-e-a-l-l-y wanted me. Next, the maitre'd was quite taken, and I concluded I must be really hot. When the waiter appeared equally infatuated, I thought, *I am smokin' tonight.* My travel companions also showed signs of being enthralled, and I concluded that I had it going on. I was hot, hot, hot.

Bantering with the waiter, my travel partners revealed that we were from Oklahoma. Indian Territory came up in the conversation, at which time the waiter looked at me and said "Ah ha," like that explained everything. This was mystifying to me until later in my hotel room when I discovered vivid red stripes on my cheeks. As I re-traced the events of the evening, each incident took on new meaning. Although embarrassed that I looked like a woman prepped for a war dance, I was mostly disappointed about not being so hot after all.

That was when I still cared about whether I was hot or not. I don't invest much in my appearance anymore. I go to coffee in pajamas with unkempt hair representative of a mop. About once a week I care what I look like. The rest of the time I don't. There is freedom in that—a burden lifted.

What we have here is a failure to give a crap. I'm conflicted on whether that is where I want to be, especially since I aspire to have game. Well, maybe I don't aspire to have game. Then again, yes, I do. I want to be vintage with game. Or maybe just vintage. Or maybe neither. Or maybe both. I'm conflicted.

I like to think this newfound indifference to appearance is the result of becoming a fully self-actualized woman; however, it may be that I've given up on something that's not going to happen anymore no matter what I do. Whatever the motive, I no longer aspire to look youthful, and I'm not one to adopt a glamourous style or a sultry one that suggests a safari fight broke out in my closet. But I'm not into simplicity squared and neatness on the level of a politician's wife either. When age inflicts its consequences, I fight the good fight, but I'm more interested in being a fascinating old gal than representing an up-to-date, polished, coordinated fashion plate.

* * *

My daughter helps me keep reasonably current. Women in Tulsa were still wearing hose when bare legs came into vogue in California. Finding it profoundly embarrassing when her mother wore hose, she mandated I not even think about packing a pair when I came to see her. This trend was a problem for my generation. We counted on hose to disguise defects so we could operate under the delusion that we still had great legs. Eventually, we old gals realized that abandoning hose was freedom. However, this produced a proliferation of orange-legged women giving off the unpleasant scent of tanners marketed as having no scent.

We've all done it. I had my body spray tanned for a luau party only to wake up in a Dallas hotel orange all over the day of the party. A scrubbing shower could not eliminate the orange. Instead, it produced red blotches, so at the luau my skin matched my orange and red lei.

* * *

Out-dated style contributes to the perception of older generations as stodgy and feeds the interpretation of us as irrelevant. This doesn't mean we should adopt the fads of the young, who are quite naked and clearly looking to get laid, but we can acknowledge some trends without looking foolish. For example, with the young, matchy-matchy is out. This contrasts with our inclination to adopt a put-together look that suggests we've been redecorated. Today, it is best not to appear redecorated.

I try to be open-minded about the youthful trends of sloppiness and mutilated bodies. It doesn't bother me to see mutilation at the county fair. It worries me, though, when it is on my estate planner's paralegal, and I don't like a mohawk, tattoos, and piercings on the guy who makes my cappuccino. I need to feel that anyone involved in my business or food is using good judgment and is statistically unlikely to have hepatitis.

The teller at my bank had a row of piercings running down each ear, a rattlesnake tattoo around her neck, and black nail polish with a skull painted on a middle finger. This was a tad distracting. It wasn't Halloween, so I wondered if she was a pirate and if the person who hired her was mentally unstable. She gave me the right bills, but when she said "Have a nice day," I suspected she really meant "Fuck you very much." I considered that the skull on her middle digit might be her way of giving me the finger. Maybe not. Perhaps she was a sweet young thing who genuinely wanted me to have a nice day. In that case, I worry about her and what kind of boyfriend she has, and I already have enough to worry about.

At work I had to enforce a corporate dress code. This meant reining in young women determined to expose pierced tummies, cleavage, tattoos, bras, and the back straps of thongs that peek out of waistbands and cause men to lose their train of thought. Men are easily distracted. I observed a conference room full of them lose their minds over a leopard print top with serious cleavage. Believing they'd died and gone to heaven, the guys didn't hear a word the woman said and never did recover. They talk about it to this day. Remember when . . .

Perhaps we should maintain our sense of humor when it comes to the young so they will do the same with us. Rather than continue to make fun of his young grandson who wore his pants so low that his underwear showed and the crotch struck the young man almost at his knees, an elderly man designed an intervention. He conspired with other relatives to wear their pants low slung with underwear revealed to a family dinner. Some even went so far as to show some butt crack. Small children, women, and old folks waddled around with pant crotches almost down to their knees. Baby diapers were even riding low. This was a hoot and photos recorded the event, eventually finding their way into photo albums, frames on pianos and fireplaces, and the Internet.

My generation had sound reasons for our conventional appearance. In the career arena, women needed every edge they could get. An accounting manager in the seventies lamented to me that he couldn't send a brilliant female co-worker to a meeting because she dressed like a person going to Fiji on vacation. So he sent me instead. "I can't send her," he explained. "Who knows what she'll wear? The guys will make fun of me." You have to appreciate his predicament. Men are brutal with their joshing.

It was hard enough for women to be taken seriously in those days without adding appearance issues to the mix. A professional look was vital. Our dress requirements were determined by men. Over time, we found our voice, realized our strength, took the power, and influenced how we were "allowed" to dress. In the seventies, we protested the ban on pant suits, and it was lifted. Later the requirement to wear hose was eliminated. We voluntarily gave up girdles, although we are still victims of pointy-toed shoes and heels so high that we walk like praying mantises. Men love women in heels, but do they know that praying mantises kill their partners after mating?

We are not our mother's compliant generation, forced to realize progress through gentle manipulation so as not to rock the boat. Nor do we look like them, or even ourselves a few decades back. Some of us have saucy leopard print shoes, fitness memberships, and purposeful work. Others have abandoned makeup routines, embraced simple haircuts, and cast aside high heels, fashion, and careers for matters of personal satisfaction and social importance. Either way, we are trailblazers again—redefining aging.

Standing on the shoulders of generations of women before us, we are committed to shepherding those who follow. We may not "get" the tattoo and piercing mentality of our protégés, the appeal of a woman's butt crack, or the acceptance of a muffin top that bursts forth from low cut jeans, but we will support our mutilated, exposed successors with vigor and savage determination.

* * *

In my fifties, times were good. Those were glory days. Although there were traumatic losses during that period, optimism resembling an adolescent hopefulness prevailed. My career peaked, and I was well past the menopausal hot flashes so intense that they made my glasses steam over. I was still a high-energy, bony-ass woman dressed in fantastic clothes and traveling to interesting places. And I was productive beyond belief.

The angry resignation that followed in my sixties was unforeseen, but it was lurking there. It invaded my world insidiously. My emerging disinterest in fitness and appearance contributed to that misadventure. I looked in the mirror one day and wondered, *Who is this old lady? Perhaps I look better from the back.* Probably not. Back fat. Tush droop. A Rubenesque waffle woman. Despair. I was on a roller coaster. The loving myself in the mirror the day before, when I was so blissfully golden that I blew myself a kiss, turned to disgust, and I wondered if I was bipolar.

I'm stronger today, but I continue to waver. One day I might stare at myself in the mirror in wonder and marvel at the contrast of the sturdiness and power within with the etched manifestation of age on the face staring back at me. I've touched that mirror to feel the realness of the woman there and considered how grateful I am to go on an aging journey with this creature. On another day, I look at her and wonder again if perhaps I look better from the back.

I like to think I still have game, but I waver on that, too. "Yes, you have game. No, you don't. Yes, you do. No. Yes. No." When I feel like I have no game, it helps to recall this incident. I joined my coffee group after a long absence while visiting *Thing I* and *Thing II* in California. Someone asked how the trip went. I responded by singing the Smokey the Bear song, which was the reigning infatuation of *The Things*. My coffee mates listened intently. One of the men stared at me for some time afterward and eventually said, "I want you so-o-o-o bad." You see, sometimes I do have game.

At this stage, the key to having game is to cover things up. When an obnoxious vein popped up on my calf one day, I was shocked. A few weeks earlier I noticed cellulite on my shoulders. How weird is that? This meant more body parts had to be covered up. Bummer. I would soon be in a burka. It is impossible to have game in a burka.

Hiding flaws is a strategic endeavor. When a man puts his arm around my waist, I stretch sideways and lean into him hard. This eliminates the roll of fat his hand might discover above my waistband, the one visually disguised by a billowing top purchased in a maternity department. However, if a man creeps me out, I consider the fat appendage an asset in the category of tear gas. This is rarely effective, though. Creepy guys don't care if you have excessive belly fat—or head lice or anything else.

Two words help me cope. *Oh well.* I say them to myself out loud when I notice a body issue, usually after a swear word or two. Potent medicine is dispensed through a well-timed

Oh well. It doesn't give me game, but it promotes acceptance, and that gives me game—sort of.

Another coping mechanism is to interpret degrading body changes as patina. Copper takes on a green tone as it weathers, which many consider beautiful. When decorating homes, I tell people that little scratches, marks, and dents on furniture and accessories add character. These defects are patina—evidence of history. They prove that the item has endured and is valued, used, and beautifully flawed. Cosmetic flaws on bodies can be interpreted this way. Patina is achievable while perfection is a hopeless objective that sucks the life out of a person. A new version of beauty can be interpreted by embracing the concept of patina.

It would be misguided, though, to suggest that all visible signs of aging are beautiful. They are not. But they are organic and pure. Your best bet is to class it up a bit, which in general means "cover that up." Classiness is the mark of a refined, mature woman. It is our edge. The young rarely achieve that level of sophistication.

Although I'm all up for doing anything a person can do to look good, I'm less preoccupied with how I look these days. I bought a maternity top for my class reunion rather than lose weight. I tried Botox and filler, but they are expensive and only last as long as tornado season. There are more important things to do with money than plumping up my face. And I have other things to worry about like the people who live in my attic and steal my slippers and raid my refrigerator—and men on motorcycles.

I try to embrace with grace and acceptance the changes that reflect my longevity, and I've been relatively successful at that, except for my tummy. I've been romancing it some, so I don't hate it. At times I feel as though I've at least resigned myself to it with my *Oh well* tactic. But, to be honest, I hate it. And I'm still trying to decide if I care about the state of my elbows. As Nora Ephron said, "If your elbows faced forward, you would kill yourself."

The stomach faces forward, so it is a constant reminder of a battle lost. Accepting bodily changes is never simple, but it gets easier when you focus on mattering. No one cares about my tummy but me. Only me. And most everyone else has one. I used to snuggle up to guys on the dance floor. Now we bump bellies. *Oh well.*

* * *

In spite of all protestations, my girlfriends and I are still prisoners of how we look, so we occasionally set out to prove we still have game. This requires a major overhaul. Having game is a lot of work. We dress up in a desperate attempt to *not* look like Bea Arthur and make an excursion into the Tulsa night scene. We do this to prove we've still got "it," whatever "it" is, even though we don't want "it."

I look forward to when what I look like doesn't matter. I can cut my hair, go gray, wear glasses, and avoid makeup. That time will come. For now, I'm compelled to occasionally set out to prove I've got game. After I do that, I spend days recuperating because I don't have that much game. *Oh well.*

Most likely, we don't have "it" anymore anyway. However, enough determined old men, somewhat resembling George Costanza, have hopeful visions of rolling a woman in flour and targeting the wet spots. With that frame of reference, they harbor grand illusions that we still have "it." We flirt with these determined fellows who, when turned down for a dance, or anything else, are prone to say, "Fine, I'll ask you again when you're rested." We feed their egos as they flatter us, a *quid pro quo* type of action, all the while staving off serious advances.

Our frame of mind is limited to having fun. Although, in general, we believe that you can never have too much fun, we have occasionally been on the verge of doing so. Being well-seasoned, we know the consequences of that. We were reminded of this when we met a fellow who in a matter of minutes changed from Good Rob to Bad Rob and then back to Good Rob and . . . he was a mess.

We are wiser than in our younger years. We know that the good ones are married, the divorced ones are bitter and poor, and the rest just want to do our hair. We accept that man's interpretation of housework is limited to vacuuming. We recognize that music can be an irritant. Most of us have had the experience of surround sound so loud it caused our sternums to vibrate. We've learned it's best to call AAA to rescue us from car trouble and to use the Internet to help us buy a car rather than feed a man three times a day. And we celebrate that we no longer have to worry that we might get pregnant while helping our guy give up smoking.

So at this stage in our lives, around nine-thirty we head home for a connection with our vibrators—or not. Probably not. "It" is a lot of trouble, and we have a line dancing class at the senior center in the morning where we rumba, samba, cha-cha, charleston, salsa, and do the hokey pokey. Apparently, the hokey pokey *is* what it's all about.

* * *

In my younger years, I tortured myself in uncomfortable clothes and shoes just to look good. Today, I've shifted from the corporate image to that of a writer. I'm no longer a good capitalist. I rarely shop for clothes. In fact, I'm a bit of a coffee shop slouch, but you won't find me dressed in float trip clothes or the American uniform of jeans and tennis shoes. They hold no appeal for me. I'm full of contradictions about how I look. I care. I don't care. I'm classy. I'm a slouch. I'm a mess. Maybe I *am* bipolar.

My goal these days is not to avoid looking old, which is futile anyway, but to simply look good for my age. I consider myself deliciously flawed. Even when bludgeoned by fluorescent lights in department store dressing rooms with their multiple mirrors that reflect old ladies looking back at me from all directions, I'm moderately successful at applying the concept of patina. I tap into the *oh well*, and distract myself with more important matters. If that doesn't work, I use sentence enhancers. "What the fuck happened here, goddamn it to hell, shit . . . son of a bitch?"

* * *

How I dress affects how I feel, and I suspect it would disturb my children if I got too sloppy. Remembering my responsibility to role-model aging for them, I step it up a bit, even adding more colorful clothes to my wardrobe.

Years ago, a professor in one of my education classes advised her students, who were aspiring teachers, to wear cheery colors on dreary days. "You won't feel like it," she said, "but do it for your students. It will make a difference in their day." That's a powerful message. How a person looks can be a positive influence on those they care about.

My signature color for years was black, but acknowledging the impact of color, I wear more of it now, even though red makes me feel like a geranium and yellow a glow stick. Sometimes I get *Project Runway* excited and wear several colors. This is a shock to friends who are acclimated to my black inclinations. They call me a piñata and threaten to whack me with a stick. A multi-colored outfit prompted one of them to describe me as three-quarters of a donkey cart. Sometimes I wear a print so outrageous it looks as though I've been upholstered, and old men threaten to sit on me.

Color has a mystical sway on the psyche. When Mother was in a nursing home, a pleasant feeling swept over me each time I entered her room to find her dressed in her signature color. It was a soft blue that made her glow and complemented her blue eyes and silver hair the texture of cotton candy. Someday, when my children visit my nursing home, I will be shining and sparkling to the best of my ability. I may even wear red shoes. I will do that for them.

Since I rarely wear makeup these days, my three-year-old granddaughter was taken aback one day when I was decked out for a flight back to Tulsa. I had slobbed around the entire visit (managing children leaves little time for self-grooming). Mystified at my new look, she stared at me intently. She asked, "GoGo, why are you all fancy?" I told her I got all fancy to fly in an airplane. She then asked if she could get all fancy too, so I shared my makeup.

She worked herself over pretty good with an eyebrow pencil and proudly said, "GoGo, look at my eyebrows." She had drawn an array of jagged eyebrows across her forehead. I tried not to laugh at her fancy self and complimented her proliferation of eyebrows. I suggested she show them to her mother and followed along to watch the reaction. Her mom did a good job of appreciating her eyebrows without laughing outright, and the little diva and her GoGo resumed efforts to get all fancy with lipstick.

She often gets all fancy with princess dresses, heels, tiaras, tutus and all kinds of fussy garb. When I was a child, Disneyland didn't exist and I was tiptoeing around the farmyard barefoot trying to avoid chicken poop and four brothers. So I never aspired to being a princess. Instead, I marveled at puffy, lacy dresses and Mary Jane shoes in the Sears catalogue and dreamed of having them for my own— a dream unfulfilled. I wore plaid dresses and shoes so unremarkable that I have no memory of them.

As an adult, though, I've had my days of high fashion and ridiculously extensive wardrobes. Now I dress mostly for comfort and simplicity. My red heels are lower these days than the high ones I wore during the disco era, and I don't wear them as often as I used to, but it is always delightful to see them on the shelf in my closet.

I'm back and forth on whether I have game or not, but I do know this. I may not look any better from the back than I do from the front, but I've still got nice eyebrows. And I've got moxie. I can't predict the future of my eyebrows or anything else, but regardless of what I look like, I plan to keep my moxie forever, no matter what happens.

chapter 16

SOMETIMES I DO THINGS I SHOUDN'T

Don't call me if you get thrown in jail.

Someone once said that no one's life is ever wasted because a life can always serve as a bad example. For me, this may apply because sometimes I do things I shouldn't. There is a fine line between setting a bad example and showing how to live life full out.

After reporting my adventures to my children, they sometimes respond, "And how old are you people?" Occasionally they say, "Don't call me if you get thrown in jail," a threat I often made to them in their spirited teenage years. When I texted my daughter about a food fight in a sushi bar, she responded, "Don't make me come over there." Each time I hear these remarks, I know I've redeemed myself from the doldrums of a few years back. I also know that eliciting such responses from my children is proof that they are paying attention and that I am still relevant, at least in some sense of the word.

I suspect my behavior causes them some anxiety. No longer restricted by a professional reputation, corporate requirements, or worries about embarrassing my mother, I'm a bit of an eccentric rebel these days. The older I get, the less societal requirements influence my behavior. I'm free! I'm free! It is possible, though, that I am in need of a freedom intervention.

Being old gives people the license to do things they didn't have the courage to do in younger years. As we age, we have less and less to lose, and we can get by with things. Although I have no plans to jump out of a perfectly good airplane or ride to the top of Pikes Peak on a Harley driven by some fellow called Mad Moose, my rebel spirit has blossomed. I wrote a fiction piece about that. It is not based on my past. It is based on my future.

SOMETIMES MAVIS DOES THINGS
SHE SHOULDN'T

Mavis squirms in the seat of her Lexus as she watches traffic backing up. The street light, disabled by a passing thunderstorm, flashes red, and every driver must stop and maneuver through a helter-skelter mess of vehicles.

A police car moseys through the intersection. Because of its leisurely pace, Mavis concludes that the policemen inside have nothing better to do than direct traffic. It irritates her that they do not. She always wanted to direct traffic.

Mavis is a "can do" gal. Before retirement, she ran a company where she didn't tolerate inaction when bad things happened to customers or employees. She would say, "Do something—even if it's wrong." She wanted to put "dammit" on the end of that sentence but, of course, she couldn't do that. Corporate America frowns on such things. In her mind, those policemen had an obligation to *do something* about the traffic backup, dammit.

Now retired, Mavis enjoys not having to comply with workplace restrictions or to worry about her reputation. As a result, she's become a bit of a pistol. She is doing a lot of things she shouldn't these days. When she tells her children about them, they often say "Don't call me if you get thrown in jail," something she said to them when they were spirited teenagers.

Mavis eases her way up to the light as traffic allows while becoming more and more impatient. Although she has all day, she knows other people have somewhere to be. So when she spots a driveway just short of the intersection, she pulls in and parks, gets out, and proceeds to the middle of the intersection.

Surely a strange sight—an old lady in yoga wear with hair looking like a fright wig—Mavis begins directing traffic. She's awkward at first but soon masters the flow of the process and orders cars this way and that with abandon. The rhythm of movements required to direct traffic remind her of disco dancing back in 1978. Drivers wave in appreciation. Some honk. Most are laughing.

A police car pulls up and two cops approach. The look of amusement on their faces belies their authoritative demeanor.

"Ma'm, you can't do this."

"Why not?"

"It's against the law."

"Well, you do it then."

Mavis considers tacking "dammit" on the end of her proposal. She doesn't only because one of the officers reminds her of her grandson. She ignores them and continues waving cars through the intersection, her moves now crisp and sure. She wishes she had a whistle. Drivers take note of the confrontation, and honking escalates. The police shift their weight from foot to foot. They really don't want to arrest this old woman, but they move in closer.

While keeping her eyes on the task at hand, Mavis asks, "You are not going to tase me, are you?" Her arm swirls in broad circles, skillfully guiding drivers on their way in an orderly manner.

"No, we wouldn't do that."

Both they and Mavis know that would not be necessary. The officers could easily lift her tiny frame by the arms and carry her off with her feet circling as though she were riding a bicycle, and they are prepared to do so. Mavis senses this, stares belligerently at them for a moment, then turns and stomps toward her car as drivers honk like crazy. The officers are relieved. The drivers are aggravated. Horns blare.

She considers how things might have ended differently. A policeman could have said, "Have a seat. Watch your head." Or she could have been loaded into an ambulance with one of them asking, "Ma'am, can you describe the car that hit you? Ma'am? Ma'am?"

Mavis is disappointed that her dissidence was cut short, but she smiles as she puts the key in the ignition. She always wanted to direct traffic, and she thinks about how sometimes she does things she shouldn't. Mavis makes a mental note to pick up a whistle the next time she goes to the store.

When it comes to doing things I shouldn't, I'm encouraged by friends who are my kind of crazy. To convey the tone of our interactions, I wrote about a typical coffee session. Although fictional, it is based on real experiences with real people and includes tidbits from several coffees of old folks. I call them *The What Just Happened Gang*.

Sam arrived early at The Crescent Coffee Shop and scored a table for six. He is known for his nasal incontinence, which means, when he laughs, coffee comes out of his nose. Emma showed up sporting a new cane that stands up all by itself. The group suspects it contains a taser.

Bonnie, the group's voice of reason, suggested to Emma that she sit in her chair *normal.* She fell out of it last time and flailed around on the floor like a turtle on its back for some time before helpers got her up. Sam offered to hold Emma in place and slid his arm around her. Emma stomped his foot with her cane. He reacted as though he'd been tased.

As Godfrey shuffled in late, the group hummed the Alfred Hitchcock Show theme song, which perfectly matched his lumbering pace. He wore a broad-brimmed hat and carried an umbrella since Wanda throws pecans and yogurt at him.

Wally, who can't hear so well but refuses to wear hearing aids, showed up. He lives in a world of *What just happened?* His primary contribution to conversations is "WHAT?"

Emma gave a report on her thyroid.

Sam gave a report on his thyroid.

Wanda arrived late wearing silver knee-high boots, àla Wonder Woman style.

Godfrey gave a report on his thyroid.

Wanda reported she had no thyroid—or ovaries.

Wally picked up on "ovaries" and said, "WHAT?"

Sam reported he had a leaky carburetor, and he wasn't talking about his car.

To steer the discussion away from medical issues, Bonnie said, "Speaking of sex." (She insists she is not bossy. She is a leader.) Wally picked up on "sex" and said, "WHAT?"

To comply with Bonnie's suggestion, Sam told a joke about an old couple who had sex every Sunday to the pace of church bells ringing. The old fellow died one morning when an ice cream truck went by. Everyone laughed except Wally who wondered, *What just happened?*

Wanda revealed that she missed her ex-husband who ran off with a waitress who got her toe stuck in a bathtub faucet. She said, "My ex is a consummate rescuer." No one argued the point.

Wanda told a joke. Everyone laughed, except Wally. Hoping to be on topic, although he had no clue what the topic was, he reported, "I watched Harrison Ford pierce Jimmy Fallon's ear on television last night." The group suggested he rethink his DVR selections. He said, "WHAT?" Emma asked, "What is a DVR?"

Bonnie said, "Judge Judy told some guy he wouldn't be any stupider if someone cut his head off—or was that Dr. Phil, or Maury? Whatever." Godfrey suggested she rethink her DVR selections and gave an update on the reality show *Finding Sasquatch*, which he believed meant scientists were on the verge of a watershed scientific breakthrough.

Wanda, who has a compulsion to hide things, hid Emma's purse when she went for more coffee. She also has a compulsion to throw things, and she threw a pecan at Godfrey. It landed on his hat. Knowing there would be another, he ignored it.

Wanda announced that she was dating a Vietnam vet who had convinced her that weed was a condiment. He had some powerful stuff that made her teeth feel big.

Bonnie advised the group that gospel singers on The Lawrence Welk Show once sang *One Toke Over the Line, Sweet Jesus* on television. It was debated whether Welk or the singers knew what the song was about. Wanda Googled the show on her phone and passed it around. Godfrey hid the phone in the belt line of his pants.

A sweet potato nugget whizzed by Wanda's head, smacked against the wall, and fell to the floor. No one reacted, probably because it was not that unusual—a payback of some sort. The incident reminded them of being kicked out of The Mulberry Street Coffee Shop.

Wanda reported that she and her Vietnam vet boyfriend ate the best raisins in the universe and a whole box of Fruit Loops after their movie date Saturday night.

Wally recounted a story about a man with a wooden leg being eaten alive by termites, a matter he had reported at several previous coffees. Picking up on the group's lack of interest, he turned his attention to his empty plate, which a few minutes ago held a cinnamon roll the size of a small dog. He stared at the plate intently for an awkward moment and then said, "My doctor warned me that if I keep eating sugar, I could end up in a diabetic coma."

This inspired several other "my doctor told me" stories from the group followed by Godfrey giving a report on his colonoscopy. Knowing everyone in the group had had a colonoscopy, Bonnie said, "Speaking of sex."

The group spoke about sex.

People at the next table eavesdropped.

People at the next table left.

People at another nearby table left.

Emma tore the place up looking for her purse.

Wanda's phone vibrated and slipped down Godfrey's pants. As he struggled to retrieve it, Wanda offered to help which caused the two to circle the table twice. Godfrey shook his right leg intermittently until the phone fell to the floor. Sam retrieved it and put it in his pants.

Bonnie was embarrassed by this behavior and suggested the group contemplate the world situation or the Red Dot Shoe Sale at Macy's. Wanda wondered if it included boots. Wally farted and everyone scattered while he wondered, *What just happened?*

Wanda's phone started vibrating in Sam's pants as he refilled his cup at the self-service table, which caused him to slosh coffee down the front of his khaki pants. When he returned to the table, several women offered to help dry him off. Emma had a small battery-powered fan she carried in her purse, which she couldn't find since Wanda had hidden it.

The gang regrouped. Godfrey opened his umbrella as Wanda had purchased an ample supply of yogurt. Emma realized where her purse had gone when the tune *It's a Wonderful World* reverberated from under Wanda's chair.

Wally left. Someone told him to have a nice day. He said, "WHAT?" So the goodwill message was repeated in unison by all members of the group, "HAVE A NICE DAY." He responded, "I've got other plans."

Emma, who sat in her chair *normal*, gave a weather report. Godfrey said the book he was reading was so full of flourish that it represented literary masturbation, a topic the group was about to address when Sam had a thought that excited him. "Oh, oh, oh!" he interrupted. "Grey Goose is gluten free and contains no sugar." Bonnie, always the voice of reason, reacted with her usual response to nonsensical remarks, "We are still all Unitarians, though, aren't we?"

I've sat in that coffee shop many times in the midst of young students, working people on break, and various groups of hanger outers. Probably no one in there appreciates just being there more than my coffee group pals, and it is unlikely anyone values the prospect of doing things they shouldn't more than we do.

We are approaching the age where no one is going to throw us in jail no matter what we do, short of murder. Mom was eighty and stewing over a $16 medical bill. She spent hours on the phone trying to resolve the issue. Because she couldn't hear, her end of the conversations was mostly "WHAT?" She asked me to help. Not wanting to spend precious time with her doing that, I advised her, "Don't pay it, don't talk to anyone about it, and throw any paperwork about it away." She worried this would ruin her credit or she would end up in debtors' prison. "What the hell is debtors' prison?" I asked.

Once that concept was explained, I said, "Mom, you don't need a credit rating, there is no debtors' prison, and no one is going to throw you in jail. You are old. You get to do what you want. In this case, that is nothing." Mom responded, "WHAT?"

I don't worry much these days about the consequences of potentially inappropriate but innocuous behavior. After watching a *Saturday Night Live* Christmas special in which someone hilariously humped a Christmas tree, I sensually embraced one at a senior dance party to the delight of my friends. Later I thought, *Did I just hump a Christmas tree?* The act was confirmed with a picture posted on the Internet by someone as technically proficient as I was. It was upside down. I worried the posting would damage my credit rating and enhance my reputation with old men. I told my daughter about my concerns and she asked, "And how old are you people?"

Some people become fearful and less adventuresome as they age. Others become braver like my guy friend who gave a woman in our coffee group a vibrator for her birthday. The birthday girl complained that it was so small it was as though her vibrator had a baby. Someone turned it on, and it danced around on the coffee shop table before landing in a man's lap. He reacted as though he'd stepped on a snake and then had a seizure.

How boring would life be if we were always right and proper? I even respond improperly to tornadoes these days. When the warning sirens go off, I go outside to look at it, at least until cows start swirling by.

A "shouldn't" comes from someone else's perspective. The reason I do things is because I think I should, otherwise I wouldn't do them. When self-righteous people seek to impose their inhibitions on me and stare at me like a tree full of owls when I don't meet their standards, I rebel. I don't need a credit rating, there is no debtors' prison, and I have plenty of friends who are my kind of crazy.

* * *

Risk-taking behavior intensified when my kids were raised and love was lost. An "I've got nothing to lose" state of mind set in. One of the consequences of this was that I began going on night shift patrol with law enforcement. The series of adventures this produced were intoxicating. To this day, when a patrol car is running hot, I want to hop in and ride shotgun. Even in that venue, I did things I shouldn't. When searching for Walt, a missing Alzheimer's wanderer, we located his car in a store parking lot and initiated a search. My designated section of the store included the shoe department. After locating Walt, the officers began a search for me.

In another encounter with law enforcement, I was working very late at the office when police surrounded a car in front of the building. Blaring sirens and flashing lights stirred the night, and a megaphone blasted, "Buck, show your hands." Concerned that Buck would opt to shoot it out, I left my office and headed for the back parking lot.

Rounding a corner in a dark hallway, I crashed into SWAT team members dashing to an observation window. The reaction was similar to when ET and the little girl in the movie saw each other for the first time. She screamed and then he screamed, except the SWAT team fellows didn't scream. They swore, and there ain't nothing hotter than a potty mouth in a SWAT uniform.

Shortly thereafter, as I juggled papers and a briefcase in the parking lot while unlocking the car, I accidentally pulled the pin on the alarm I carried for late night security. This produced a loud screeching noise. In a panic, I dropped it, and it rolled under the car. When the police rounded the building, guns drawn and at the ready, I was on my knees, butt in the air, reaching for the alarm.

"Ma'am, can we help you?" they asked.

"No thank you. I've got it," I said, surfacing from under the car with the screeching alarm in hand.

As I fumbled to insert the pin and gather up papers, uniformed officers stood in various manly stances looking like statues of warriors. They were captivating. I wanted to hang around for the adrenalin-fueled aftermath—similar to the winding down process involving a cigarette after sex—but Buck showed no signs of giving up. So I headed home to dream of badges, guns, bullhorns, SWAT gear, flashing blue lights, and other things I probably shouldn't.

* * *

I generally avoided doing things I shouldn't in the office setting, but in a blues bar in Kansas City, some business associates and I partied a bit too heartily to appropriately represent our conservative organization. So we panicked when the band asked us through a blaring microphone what company we were with. One of the fellows in our group did something he shouldn't and yelled out the name of our fiercest competitor, after which we partied on.

Nightclub venues are teeming with people being rude and inconsiderate. I follow my son around to such places when he plays in bands. No matter where I position myself, someone invariably stands in front of me blocking my view. I tap them on the shoulder and tell them someone threw up where they are standing.

Clubs and parties are ideal places to do things you shouldn't. A guy I know puts peanut butter between the heel and sole of his shoe for parties and sits around with his leg crossed. Invariably someone points out something on his shoe. He fakes surprise, puts his finger in it, and tastes it. This is his signature party move. Someday people will talk about it at his funeral, which makes me wonder what will be said at mine. I hope people tell stories about the things I did that I shouldn't, and it occurs to me that it would be nice if someone swore at my funeral.

* * *

I don't do things I shouldn't around boyfriends anymore because I don't have boyfriends anymore. I had my moments, though. If a boyfriend messed with me, I got even by introducing Q & A after sex. If one tried to start an argument, he was told to talk to the hand. One asshole who possessed the sensitivity of a trained assassin got played like a fine guitar until my girlfriends, in a glorious woman-to-woman intervention, convinced me of a potential homicidal outcome. In spite of these episodes, I was typically generous and devoted to my men as demonstrated by the fact that I hung a large chrome clock above the toilet tank in the bathroom—one that reflects things and makes them look larger than they actually are.

I once wore a fur coat over a bikini, a garter belt, fishnet hose, four-inch heels, and strategically placed bows to a boyfriend's house for his birthday. I was careful not to speed. Any self-respecting policeman would have had me step out of the car so his car-cam could get a shot for the entertainment of buddies and dispatchers. It would have been one of those "you're not going to believe this" moments. The smile on my boyfriend's face when he opened the door and I said, "Happy birthday, baby," was worth the risk. Later, I asked him if he would buy me a car.

Although I'm not active in the area of romance these days, I still think about things I shouldn't. Thoughts revolve mostly around pirates, men in uniform, and bomb squad robots. The appeal of pirates surfaced after I observed an actor dressed as Johnny Depp's character, Captain Jack, at a children's birthday party. As he sword fought with children, it occurred to me that I would like to straddle him in the bowels of a ship. I thought something I shouldn't.

The attraction to men in uniform began initially at a weekend boot camp at a military base. This was part of a program to give citizens a taste of what it is like to be a soldier. It was there that a bunch of overweight VIPs, myself included, were greeted by a cute, young drill sergeant with shiny, sparkly eyes who boarded the bus that delivered us and yelled, "You've got three minutes to get off this bus, and one of them is already gone."

We sported heavy military backpacks of some sort, which caused some participants to step off the bus and continue downward until their faces reached the pavement. This debacle reflected the level of military unreadiness of our group and royally entertained the drill instructor. We were soon in pushup mode, which had most of us looking like beached whales as the sergeant stood over us yelling.

As I stood at attention, the youthful drill sergeant got into my personal space and yelled, "Where are you from, soldier?" I started to answer when he barked, "It doesn't matter where you're from. You're in the Army now." His dark brown eyes blazed, but his youthful fervor overcame me. He reminded me of my son, who was about his age, and I said, "You are just to-o-o-o cute."

He maintained his composure, I thought, but one of my cohorts told me the sergeant stood behind our ragtag troop of hapless VIP soldiers and laughed himself silly before moving on to terrorize another pathetic pretend soldier. Sadly for me, this experience triggered an attraction to men in uniform that grew to include mall security guards, UPS delivery men, and men in forest ranger shirts.

The appeal of men in uniform collided with my love of accessories when the drill sergeant handed me dog tags. I exclaimed excitedly, "Accessories!" Later, a very buff soldier gave me heavy leather gloves so I wouldn't burn my hands while firing shells out of a training tank. I said, "Accessories!" While touring a mess hall, a soldier handed me a hat and rubber gloves. I exclaimed, "Accessories!"

On another military tour, a drop-dead gorgeous Top Gun Navy pilot in the San Diego ship yards put a flight vest and pilot's hat on me. I said, "Accessories!" These experiences not only inspired a preoccupation with men in uniform, they provoked a propensity to see things as accessories that are not really accessories. When my boyfriend whipped out a condom, I may have ruined the moment, but I couldn't help myself. I had to say it. Sometimes I say things I shouldn't, and I do love accessories.

* * *

Excessively irreverent, I tell jokes I shouldn't. My favorite is about the remote Facarwi tribe who lived in a far away place. They got their name because they were nomads. Every morning when they stepped outside of their tents, they said, "Where the fuck are we?"

Then there is the chicken joke about the Oklahoma man hustling a waitress in New York City. I won't tell it here because it is insulting to chickens, but I get braver about such things as I age. I don't want to be an old person in a nursing home some day who looks back and regrets that I didn't do the crazy things I wanted to because I didn't have the guts to do them.

Jerry Jeff Walker, an old Texas country entertainer of the outlaw sort, sang about a cowboy out West who tended cattle as he read letters from his love and friends back East. In every letter they begged him to come home. They told him he was crazy out there.

Standing guard over a herd of settling cattle in the moonlight in Montana, he read one of those letters and contemplated a response, which is reflected in the song's chorus. The lyrics wax poetically about the northern lights, a hawk on the wing, the majesty of mountains, and old Camp Cookie singing. He folded the letter, put it in his pocket, and looked out over the moonlit landscape. Shaking his head, he felt sorry for those Easterners because he knew without a doubt that they were crazy out there.

People might think you are crazy when you hump a Christmas tree, but it has been said that one out of four people is mentally unbalanced. If you look around and you don't see a crazy person, you might be it. Or perhaps you reframed aging and got your moxie back.

Doing things you shouldn't may cause others to say, "And how old are you people?" Or "Don't call me if you end up in jail." Or "Don't make me come over there." But remembrances of such actions can turn the tide when you need it most. Someday they can even spice up your funeral.

When I'm wearing red heels and smokin', anything can happen because I've got moxie.

> A country boy attempted to hustle a waitress in New York City. He was having no success.
>
> Finally, he asked her, "Why won't you go out with me?"
>
> She said, "I heard about you country boys doing it with sheep and pigs and chickens."
>
> Stunned, he exclaimed, "CHICKENS?"

Sometimes I tell jokes I shouldn't.

chapter 17

PASSION, PURPOSE, AND BLISS

Doing what you were born to do:
"The two most important days in your life are
the day you were born and the day you
figured out why." . . . Mark Twain.

When I was in my mid-sixties funk and people asked what I did, I joked, "I'm training for the Olympics." I had no sense of purpose or passion, and simply saying I was retired struck me as too bland for my nature—an answer wrapped up in nothingness. So I came up with the Olympics line, a distraction from the reality of my hollow self.

Whether or not you begin to disappear at sixty is primarily determined by whether or not you have a passion for something. I knew I didn't want to be one of those old people living in the glory of the past, telling the same old stories over and over, and boring everyone into oblivion. However, I was headed in that direction.

After The California Crash, I realized that if I accepted irrelevance, I would be irrelevant. To have moxie, living a purposeful life is required. Without purpose, I am seduced into preoccupation with the past and the downside of the present—which includes growing old. The awareness I gained from my recovery revealed that passion is the path to purpose and to mattering.

Passion can mean different things to different people. It is whatever lights you up. For some it is a hobby, a sport, volunteering, travel, church, collecting, being a grandparent or a caretaker, or a host of other things. Any of those things can be shared with others in a way that makes a difference and promotes a sense of purpose. When Dr. Amy encouraged me to conquer the technology problems that stood in the way of my dream of writing, she put me on the path to realizing my passion.

"What's up?" Dr. Amy asked.

"I'm a technical idiot."

"Is that a problem?"

"Well, y-e-a-h. I spend too much time asking myself, 'Is this thing on?' Operating a computer requires the aptitude of an aircraft controller. I cannot access pictures of my grandchildren. I can't write. I can't email or impress my Oklahoma friends by posting online pictures of an Iowa prime rib the size of a platter. In today's world with all this technology, I'm now a handicapped person." Dr. Amy suggested that an *Apple* computer and their support package might resolve my problems with technology.

I was desperate. So, in spite of severe reservations, I purchased an *Apple* computer and a confusing array of requisite wires, equipment, and incidentals. All this was necessary so the computer could be "configured," a computer term for getting gadgets hooked up together so everything "articulates," a computer term for devices communicating with each other "wirelessly," a computer term for no cords, although there are cords. Many of them.

I was in over my head, so I asked "the child" who sold me this paraphernalia, "Who can set this up?" He assured me I could do it. I didn't believe him, so the equipment sat in boxes in my kitchen for weeks.

This was right after the California incident, and I was still emotionally fragile. I knew the odds of my successfully "configuring" anything were slim to none. With my passion for writing so close, the fear of it dissipating was potent. If I could not master this computer, I might end up in a permanent fetal position having fuzzy dreams about purple unicorns doing the paso doble among clouds garnished with glitter swirling on my bedroom ceiling.

Finally, one day I ate all the bacon I wanted and mustered enough courage to by god install a computer. Introducing a concept foreign to me—patience—I set about the task and installed my new *Apple* laptop, some wireless thingy, and a printer. In the process, I managed my way through the intricacies of password jungles and solved at least some of the mysteries surrounding a modem, although I never did know what a modem was or what it did. I still don't.

I did all this in four hours with nine help desk calls. Finally finished, I was astute enough to realize there were missing cords, and I called the help desk to report the problem.

After a pregnant pause, the young fellow on the phone, who by this time had an intimate connection with me, said in an exceptionally slow and precise manner:

"Mrs. Hanna, i-t i-s w-i-r-e-l-e-s-s."

"Oh. Okay, thank you."

This was not the only embarrassing part of the installation. I didn't know the dot at the top of the computer screen was a camera, so it was a shock during the installation process to suddenly see myself pop up on the screen in faded jammies, hair resembling a cat toy, and no makeup. Although the reflection didn't reveal my gray and navy striped knee socks, it was not flattering. The angle was all wrong. The camera focused on my neck, for god's sake, and it made my nose look big. The lighting was horrible. Worst of all, there was cleavage, which generated severe panic, the kind that sets off the fight or flight response. I was on the world-wide web with cleavage, looking like a slovenly trollop. Undiscriminating men all over the world would be wanting me.

Panic stricken, I rushed to the bedroom to fix up in order to appeal to the more discriminating males. After regrouping, I reconciled with the computer, adjusted the screen for a better angle, softened the lighting, smiled pleasantly, and reported the "Yikes! I'm on the Internet" problem to a help desk child who assured me no one saw it but me. "But I'm all fixed up now," I said. I now have tape over that dot. I don't trust it. With the computer in the kitchen, someone might see me loading the dishwasher naked.

It was a long morning, but I did it! I installed a computer, and I began writing my first book that afternoon. In the following months I got my land legs. By purchasing the

Apple support package, I had access to young geniuses at the store and on the phone. I refer to them as "the children." They helped me convert from Portuguese to English, after pondering how I switched to Portuguese in the first place. Like my son in third grade when he reported he got spanked for no reason at all, I told "the children" this: "It changed for no reason at all. I didn't do nothin'."

"The children" at *Apple* were primary players in my triumph. They politely and competently answered such questions as: Where is it, how do I get into it or out of it, how do I set it up, save it, back it up, attach it, convert it, transmit it, move it around, where did it go, how do I get it back, and migrate what? They tolerated my moody disposition when frustration defeated me. When a help desk child told me to upload files to 32-bit mode, I said, "Okay, sure, like that is going to happen." A young man asked me if my cookies were activated. I wasn't going to endure any trash talk. I scolded, "W-e-l-l! Aren't you the little rascal."

"The children" on the help desk keep a file on all calls. What is in mine must be good. When they talk to me, they smile with their voices. If a call goes on too long and I've completed the requisite daily Kegel exercises, I say, "I'm done here. I've got to get drunk now," which I shouldn't do because "the children" worry, except for one young man who said "All right!" Actually, I don't drink when frustrated. I eat bacon, but young people don't relate to that. They relate to jello shots.

When I'm overwhelmed, I tell the young person up front, "I am in a bad mood, and you are going to pay." After that revelation, the child patiently and determinedly carries me away to technology nirvana. With the support of "the children," a rally emerged wherein the world of bits and bytes was mastered, at least enough to realize my dreams.

Doing so was one of the most frustrating challenges of my life, but it was also one of the most rewarding. Now my computer entices me away from other activities the way dirt attracts little boys. When I approach, it rises up to greet me. When I leave, it haunts me—taunts me even. Getting to this point was a slow and steady process—one more tedious than wallpapering.

Once I overcame the technical distractions, I latched onto the passion of writing like a tattoo on a teenager on spring break in Mexico. In collaboration with "the children," I wrote books, incorporated photos in them, designed the covers, formed a publishing company, published books, and sold them on Amazon and Kindle. I designed business cards, bookmarks, and brochures. I learned how to do deep research through search engines. I can now cheat on word puzzles, fact check the news, and do background checks on men who like their women a little on the trashy side.

If I had set out originally to do all that, it would have been overwhelming. My initial goal was simply to become proficient enough at word processing to write. However, step by step and over time other capabilities were targeted and mastered. Each one led me to the next.

I set goals in increments of months. One month I learned word processing, then how to use search engines. Next, I focused on formatting followed by how to incorporate photos. Later graphic design was added to my repertoire. Twelve months later I was transmitting files to a book printer and formatting them for electronic books. Then the *coup d'état*. I designed my own website, hooked it up to PayPal, and sold books there. Over a period of two years, I mastered an impressive array of technical capabilities.

None of this came easy. I was frequently overwhelmed and in a constant state of frustration, but much was at stake. Determined to connect with others online, to realize my dream of writing, and to get my moxie back, I hung in, tapped into the digital world, and chased my dream with a vengeance. The digital world, which was once my enemy, saved me and became my partner in passion.

I still struggle with technology, though, and not just with a computer. I acquired a smart phone with which I accidentally took a picture of my feet the first day I got it. "A child" showed me how to post it on a social media site with the message, "I got a new phone with a camera." I believed I was on trend with such a fancy phone until nasty responses to my post implied I was an idiot.

Next, friends said I needed to update my phone greeting as it sounded like background noise in a pool hall. Perhaps I butt recorded it while at Owasso's Fishbonz Pool Hall where everyone knows my name: Marty's mom.

* * *

When I began writing, something magical happened—passion. It didn't happen all at once. I was goal-oriented at first with the perspective most unseasoned writers have that I would sell books and make money. Maybe I would be famous. Such an outcome was unlikely and that perspective was not going to generate passion. As I studied my new occupation, reality hit. I let go of those fanciful dreams and focused on the process of writing. A girl is more likely to score a gorgeous, rich, generous, sensitive boyfriend with a private jet who prances into a room like Richard Gere and who has an apartment in Paris than she is to make money on books. It was a relief to let go of that dream and turn my focus from the financial and glory aspects of writing to the creative ones. This allowed me to celebrate my passion.

This is what I learned about passion. Being passionate about something makes you feel you are enough just by being. Nothing else is needed to define you. Sharing passion with others promotes a sense of purpose, and sharing is the path to mattering. Once discovered, a passion is something you have to do because it fills you up. It is expressed without a sense of sacrifice. When engaged in your passion, everything else fades into the background, and time passes by unnoticed.

I knew I had found my passion when I thought I'd written for an hour one afternoon only to discover that several hours had passed and it was dark outside. When I began sharing that passion without thoughts of selling books and making money, the real magic kicked in. Passion gave me a powerful gift—relevance.

That, in turn, shed a fresh light on triumph. I re-defined success as: *I wrote it, I shared it, and someone enjoyed it.* That's enough. That's all. That's it—success—the product of passion, and it is easily achievable. With this perspective, nothing can stand in the way of success. I know for certain I will be successful when the words flow.

Writing is a roller coaster, though. Sometimes I think it is foolhardy, that no one will be interested in what I write, and my children will view the mass of books, essays, blogs, and articles I leave after I die as Mom's folly. At other times, I feel I am creating enduring treasures, jewels to be valued for generations. Legacy. Sometimes I get discouraged and abandon writing, but not for long. I always go back. When I do, I like what I wrote, or the haze has lifted, and I see a way to make a troubled composition better.

This happens because writing is my passion. I write for hours a day in airports, coffee shops, hotels, writers' retreats, and guest rooms. I write because I have to, and when I do, time passes by unnoticed. The act of writing is a gift to those who care about me because, regardless of any end product, they revel in my delight in the process.

It is the process of writing and the purpose it promotes that produce an occasional state of bliss that lights me up. Bliss is a state of being that happens in the now, such as holding a sleeping baby, being attacked by a litter of puppies, high heels burning up a dance floor, or touching a copy of your first published book.

Gleefulness overtook me when a box of my first book arrived. I tore it open like a kid with a present, held a book, gazed at my name as the author, and said out loud, "Wow!" It hit me then. *I am published.* I flipped through the pages and marveled at the photos, chapter titles, and format. I hugged the book, shivered, and had a Ginger Rogers moment as I did a happy dance in my garage. It was bliss.

More books followed. I became consumed with writing and sharing. Shortly after sending a copy of my first book to Dr. Amy, I received an email from her that said, "I'm impressed. Good for you." When I dropped off the second one, she responded, "I'm reveling in your awesomeness." Another book was delivered, and she said, "Girl, you are on fire!" I was, and I did all that without taking any medication. I worry that after I drop off this book she will say, "Call me for an appointment," after which she will suggest some serious medication.

Writing is not just a creative experience. It is a craft. Recognizing this, I became determined to master the craft. I took college courses on writing, attended seminars and workshops all over the country, and participated in writers' conferences. I read a plethora of books on writing, studied the publishing business, joined writers' groups, participated in critique groups, and sought out writers' blogs. Soon I was winning writing contests. Five years later I was judging them. I share those experiences by conducting workshops on writing and aging.

> Once you recognize within yourself a hunger for something beyond just continuing, once you taste even the possibility of touching the meaning in your life, you can never be completely content with just going through the motions. . .Oriah Mountain Dreamer, from *The Invitation*.

Some people never experience the hunger. They unconsciously spiral down and become old too soon. That was me before The Crash. When my daughter's comments forced me to face the reality of my unfortunate way in the world, a rally was sparked that introduced passion. Now I no longer feel the need to wax eloquently and make jokes about what I do by saying, "I'm training for the Olympics." Instead, I say, "I am a writer."

At first, it seemed as though I was pretending to be a writer. When I began winning awards for my writing, I became comfortable with saying so. I continue to hone my craft. While at a writers' conference in New York City, I took a break from an all-night writing marathon. An Oklahoma woman out of my element, I sat in a diner at two in the morning drinking coffee.

The Friday night crowd trailed in after a frenzied night of fun. Some patrons were decked out in nightclub garb. In contrast, I looked like a French cafe slouch in clothes comfortable enough to be classified as pajamas and hair that resembled a Muppet. I was not bothered by my appearance, though. In New York City, nothing is peculiar.

One might wonder why a sixty-something woman from Tulsa, Oklahoma, graced this setting. I was a writer, and serious writers at one time or another make a pilgrimage of sorts to New York. This quest for two a.m. coffee created a bonus adventure for this tourist who stumbled upon a flavor of the city's night life. Writers are thieves, and I decided to observe the action for the purpose of stealing ideas for a future composition. The prospects were abundant.

Exposed young girls with vocabularies embellished with the words "like" and "whatever" and blustery, cocky young men with shaved heads and baggy pants slung low enough to reveal underwear coexisted splendidly after a Friday night of partying. The women paraded by—wobbling in four-inch heels—as young men in the next booth executed the common pickup line of the testosterone-fueled night animals, "Oh my god! You are so beautiful. Oh my god!" They didn't say this to me, of course. I was still trying to lose baby fat from my firstborn child forty-eight years ago.

These comments were directed at rumpled, smudged-up, glassy-eyed unfortunates in skirts so short it appeared the girls had put on blouses and forgotten the skirts. One girl's dress was hiked up so high that the crotch of her thong was visible in the front and her bare ass in the back. Although this visual was an assault on my mind (I thought, "Gawd"), the guys were so taken by *thong girl* that they pounded the table. Unable to contain themselves, the young men rose from their seats as if their butts were filled with helium.

Following her, they omitted the "You are so beautiful," and just said, "Oh my god! Oh my god! Oh my god!"

A few gang-like fellows were so rambunctious that I expected someone would throw them out. Wondering where to hide if they started shooting, I knocked on the partition around my booth to determine if a bullet could pass through it and evaluated the prospect of squeezing myself under the table if necessary. Then I realized that a good part of the crowd behaved this way, and it was normal, at least at this hour and in this setting. No matter what happened, no one paid attention.

So I abandoned the concerned tourist role and settled in for a session of discreet observation. I did, however, make a mental note. The next time I come to New York I will explore the prospect of a more sophisticated hotel, one that leaves chocolates on my pillow and whose guests drink Grand Marnier at two in the morning.

I hung around longer than intended because my waiter, the swiper, periodically passed by at the speed of light, swooping up my half-filled coffee cup for refills. Since I'd dosed it with the required daily supplement of fiber, I had to drink each successive cup to ensure I got my thirty grams. Once accomplished, I left with a severe caffeine buzz, but not before overhearing a confounding conversation in the next booth.

A dazed young woman wearing Christmas lights as a necklace, whose head occasionally dangled perilously close to her catsup-covered french fries, lamented to her male companions that her boyfriend would be furious with her for getting so wasted. One of them comforted her by suggesting, "It'll be all right. He'll get over it." To prove his point he said, "I threw up on my girlfriend once, and she is still my girlfriend."

There I was, a mature woman from Tulsa, Oklahoma, embracing my passion and drinking coffee with the night children of New York City. In spite of their joyful exuberance, which contrasted glaringly with my mellow, pajama-clad, fiber-seeking persona, I had no envy of them. I was relevant and vital. I was a writer—a fresh label for me, a new identity that I embraced with passion.

This passion gave me purpose and helped me get my moxie back. Through it I found bliss. Through it I served. "I slept and dreamt that life was joy. I awoke and saw that life was service. I acted and behold, service was joy". . . Rabindranath Tagore

* * *

My life today has a nurturing rhythm to it. I'm crazy on writing and on life. The consequences of this are not limited to myself. Perceptions of those who observe my third-trimester aging journey are shifted by how I experience these years, and their future looks brighter.

The generational reach of the messages conveyed by how I choose to live cannot be underestimated because legacies are forever. Four-year-old Bethany carries GoGo's books around and pretends to read them. Although I'm hopeful she won't be allowed to do so until she is old enough to understand that GoGo is not always a good role model, the fact that these books exist has already made an impression.

That scenario is a far cry from the one played out when I experienced my breakdown in California. I knew my recovery was complete when one day I noticed a post on my daughter's social network page that praised one of my books. She said how proud she was of her mother. I took that in and thought, *That is how you do sixty-something.*

I am full of contradictions. I am flawed, but I'm unapologetically myself. I am strong, but sometimes fear overcomes me, and I shake like a baby rabbit in a human hand. I am grateful but haunted by the gradual decline of aging and the dread of that suddenly-one-moment incident that changes everything.

A blend of ambition and contentment churn in my head confusing me. I can't decide if I want to have game or not, but I know this. I am no longer the woman who notices a man and sucks in her stomach and stands up straighter. I am what I am. When I spot my reflection in a window and see an old woman staring at me, my disconnectedness quickly dissipates as I appreciate the sturdiness and internal power that exists behind that deeply inhabited face. I am grateful to still be here—to be the woman I have become, the one reflected in that window.

I don't know what my seventies hold in store. No doubt that time will be more challenging than the past decade. But I know this. My age is a huge factor in my life, but it is no longer the most important thing about me, and I am so over my mid-sixties crash. No matter what happens in the future, I will not go there again. I will find a way to make my seventies crazy wonderful and my eighties and nineties, too, if I get them. I've not made peace with all the pesky issues that molded me, but today I am on fire. I am relevant. I am a woman in crescendo. I've got red heels, and I am smokin'.

Books By Nikki Hanna
Available on Amazon, Kindle, and www.nikkihanna.com

OUT OF IOWA—INTO OKLAHOMA
**You Can Take the Girl Out of Iowa, but
You Can't Take the Iowa Out of the Girl**

Spanning sixty years of the author's life, this is a saucy, hilarious, and touching memoir about growing up on an Iowa farm and moving to Oklahoma. Laced with encouragement and lessons learned, it delivers a hopeful, inspirational romp through the challenges of being exposed to diverse cultures. Readers will laugh and cry. They will fall in love with Iowa, Oklahoma, and the intriguing characters in this family.

CAPTURE LIFE
Create a Biography—Leave a Legacy

This is an inspiring "how to" book that reveals how anyone can write a biography/memoir. Hanna makes a case for capturing life stories and illustrates the urgency of doing so. Five techniques are introduced that will get even the most reticent person started on a writing adventure.

Rich with invaluable details on simple and inexpensive ways to print, publish, and share stories *Capture Life* exposes the pitfalls of publishing. Helpful checklists are tools both novice and seasoned writers will appreciate.

If a story is not captured, at some point, it is lost forever. Everyone's life is interesting and worthy of preservation. Chronicling and sharing life stories creates legacy, and legacies are forever. This book shows how to accomplish that.

LEADERSHIP SAVVY
Relevant, Readable, Practical Advice
for Both New and Seasoned Leaders

This book demonstrates how to stand out as a leader, how to promote employee loyalty, and how to build an energized work force. Based on over forty years of business experience, Hanna identifies *Ten Common Leadership Mistakes*, *Ten Management Myths*, and *Five Keys to Career Success*.

RED HEELS AND SMOKIN'
How I Got My Moxie Back

If you think being sixty-something is a bummer, humorist Nikki Hanna will convince you otherwise. A playful and inspiring tale of the adventures of a woman who re-defined aging, *Red Heels and Smokin'* portrays the transitional years of the author after retirement. A gutsy, zany, and sometimes outrageous woman, Hanna is boldly candid as she dishes out amusing interpretations of her passage into what she calls the third trimester of her life— her best time.

By resurrecting the moxie that served her well in younger years, she turns a tsunami of crises that threatened to overwhelm her into an amusing story of hope and passion. The rally will have readers rooting for her recovery and perhaps strategizing to initiate one of their own.

With its wicked humor, *Red Heels and Smokin'* is an amusing and buoyant read. People under fifty will see their futures in a fresh, hopeful light, and those over fifty will find encouragement and inspiration in Hanna's astute interpretation of her aging experience—a story about how she got her moxie back.

ABOUT THE AUTHOR

When asked to describe herself in one sentence, Nikki Hanna said, "I'm a metropolitan gal who never quite reached the level of sophistication and refinement that label implies." The contradictions reflected in this description are the basis of her humorous prose. She has a B.S. Degree in Business Education and Journalism and an M.B.A. from The University of Tulsa. A retired C.P.A. and Toastmaster, Hanna has years of management experience as an executive for one of the country's largest companies. She served as a consultant on national industry task forces, as a board member for corporations, and as an advisor on curriculum development and strategic planning for educational institutions and charity organizations.

Now an author, humorist, and speaker, Hanna is dedicated to inspiring others and offers informative and entertaining programs based on her books. *Red Heels and Smokin'* and *Out of Iowa— Into Oklahoma* are memoirs that are captivating to women's groups. *Leadership Savvy* includes fresh and powerful strategies for aspiring leaders. *Capture Life* demonstrates how anyone can bestow the forever gift of legacy by sharing life stories. Her workshop *Beyond Aging Well* reveals how older people create legacy by how they construct their aging experience.

In addition to numerous awards for her poetry, essays, and short stories, Hanna is the recipient of the Oklahoma Writers' Federation's 2013 *Crème de la Crème Award*. Her books are published on Amazon/Kindle and available through her website.

Hanna lives in Tulsa, Oklahoma. She has three children who think she has become a bit of a pistol in her old age. They tell her, "Don't call me if you get thrown in jail." Her four grandchildren think she is the toy fairy and that she is somehow cosmically important. The two who live in California, *Thing I* and *Thing II*, believe she lives at the airport.

Hanna is available for customized workshops as well as for speeches, entertainment programs, and book readings.
www.nikkihanna.com

Comments on books are welcome at: neqhanna@sbcglobal.net

Made in the USA
San Bernardino, CA
15 August 2014